THE GRACE OF ARS

FATHER FREDERICK L. MILLER

THE GRACE
OF ARS

IGNATIUS PRESS   SAN FRANCISCO

Letter of His Holiness Pope Benedict XVI
Proclaiming a Year for Priests
On the 150th Anniversary of the "Dies Natalis"
of the Curé of Ars
© 2009 by Libreria Editrice Vaticana, Vatican City
Used by permission

Letter of John Paul II to All the Priests of the Church
for Holy Thursday 1986
Vatican translation reprinted by Éditions Paulines, 1986
Used by permission

Cover photographs by Adrian Chong Beng
Top: Reliquary holding the incorrupt heart of
St. John Vianney in Ars, France
Bottom: The village of Ars, France

Cover design by John Herreid

© 2010 Ignatius Press, San Francisco
All rights reserved
ISBN 978-1-58617-430-9
Library of Congress Control Number 2009935643
Printed in the United States of America ∞

I appeal to you therefore, brethren,
by the mercies of God,
to present your bodies as a living sacrifice,
holy and acceptable to God, which is
your spiritual worship.

Do not be conformed to this world
but be transformed by the renewal of your mind,
that you may prove what is the will of God,
what is good and acceptable and perfect.

—Romans 12:1–2

CONTENTS

FOREWORD

The book which you have in hand is the fruit of several pilgrimage-retreats to the holy places of Saint John Mary Vianney, the Curé of Ars, led for seminarians and priests by Father Frederick Miller, a seasoned professor of theology and spiritual director for seminarians and priests. Having conducted several pilgrimages to Ars, each including a five-day retreat, Father Miller offers us his retreat conferences in order that you and I may reap the fruit of his spiritual reflections, studying his conferences during days of retreat, either in actual pilgrimage or in mystical pilgrimage, at another place of retreat.

The publication of Father Miller's retreat conferences during the Year for Priests, proclaimed by Pope Benedict XVI to celebrate the 150th anniversary of the Death of the Curé of Ars, is especially providential. Inaugurating the Year for Priests on the Solemnity of the Sacred Heart of Jesus, the Holy Father made clear his purpose, namely, "to deepen the commitment of all priests to interior renewal for the sake of a stronger and more incisive witness to the Gospel in today's world".[1] The Year for Priests is a time of strong grace for the spiritual healing and strengthening of priests. It is also a time of strong grace for all Catholics, deepening their appreciation of the irreplaceable gift of the ordained priesthood in the Church

[1] Pope Benedict XVI, *Letter Proclaiming a Year for Priests on the 150th Anniversary of the "Dies Natalis" of the Curé of Ars*, no. 1.

ix

and leading them to pray more fervently for priests who face so many difficult challenges in fulfilling the holy mission of their vocation in the totally secularized society in which we live. In declaring the purpose of the Year for Priests, Pope Benedict XVI immediately quoted Saint John Mary Vianney's frequent and most profound description of the priesthood: "*The priesthood is the love of the heart of Jesus.*" As the Holy Father observes, the description reminds us of "the immense gift which priests represent, not only for the Church, but also for humanity itself".[2]

The retreat conferences which you are about to read are directed precisely to the purpose of the Year for Priests. They are meant to assist priests to discover anew, as on the day of their ordination, the wonderful gift of their vocation and to fortify themselves at the source of their vocation, which is the glorious pierced Heart of Jesus. As the Curé of Ars understood so well, the priest finds his identity in the Heart of Jesus the High Priest, especially as He offers up His Body and Blood as the heavenly Bread of our earthly pilgrimage in the Sacrament of the Holy Eucharist, and forgives our sins in the Sacrament of Penance. In the Holy Eucharist and Penance, above all, the priest will discover the strong grace of the Year for Priests, the grace of the interior renewal so needed to carry out the priestly mission in our day. The retreat conferences will assist the reader who is not a priest to know and love priests more, and to pray for them, so that they may meet the particular challenges of priestly life in our time.

In presenting his spiritual reflections, Father Miller comments on the special graces received through pilgrimage to Ars, the grace of a deeper understanding of: (1) the daily celebration of the Eucharistic Sacrifice as the heart of the

---

[2] Ibid., no. 1.

priestly vocation and mission; (2) the central place of all forms of the teaching office in the priestly ministry; (3) the essential relationship between the Sacraments of Penance and the Holy Eucharist; (4) priestly zeal as the inspiration for the joyful following of the evangelical counsels; (5) the essential effect of the holiness of priests upon the holiness of the flock in their care; and (6) the responsibility of the priest in organizing the works of charity. In writing about the profound interior renewal inspired in priests by pilgrimage to Ars, he concludes: "There were other graces too personal to articulate that will perhaps be recognized only in time and as various charisms unfold in the lives of priests who, following the example of the Curé of Ars, are willing to give their all for Christ and his flock." Looking at the same spiritual renewal of priests, from the perspective of "the ills of the priesthood in our times", Father Miller expresses a strong conviction that the "strong medicine" for the cure of these ills can be found in pilgrimage to Ars.

Confident in the abundant outpouring of grace through the Year for Priests and through the age-old spiritual practice of pilgrimage, it is right to view *The Grace of Ars* as a privileged instrument of grace for priests and for other faithful who are able to ponder the reflections on retreat either actually or mystically visiting the holy places of Saint John Mary Vianney who is, in the words of Pope Benedict XVI, the "model and protector of all of us, priests, and especially parish priests".[3]

Each reflection of Father Miller ponders one of the special graces received through pilgrimage to Ars, beginning with the grace of the priestly vocation itself, the call of

---

[3] Pope Benedict XVI, "Homily at Vespers Inaugurating the Year for Priests on the Solemnity of the Sacred Heart of Jesus", *L'Osservatore Romano*, Weekly Edition in English (June 24, 2009): 7.

Christ to follow Him, and priestly ordination, the consecration which sacramentally configures the priest to the person of Christ, the Head and Shepherd of God the Father's
flock in every time and place. A separate reflection is devoted
to the profound meaning of the priest's configuration to
Christ, the sacramental character by which the priest participates "in Christ's pastoral charity for his flock". The
priestly life of the Curé of Ars uncovers the great richness
of the grace conferred with priestly ordination as it is manifested in the spiritual transformation of the portion of God's
flock to which each priest is sent on mission.

Father Miller next reflects upon the evangelical counsels of poverty, chastity, and obedience in the life of the
priest. Viewing these virtues in the life of Saint John Mary
Vianney not only inspires zeal for the works of pastoral
charity in the priest but also helps him to discover the
vices which weaken and even deaden the work of God's
grace in him for the salvation of souls. Poverty teaches
the detachment from material possessions and from self,
which renders a priestly heart ever more disposed to pure
and selfless love of the flock. Through the grace of priestly
celibacy, the priest is enabled to become the spiritual father
of countless children and to make "present and visible in
the world the life that all of the redeemed will experience
in heaven after the resurrection of the dead on the last
day". Finally, the obedience practiced by the saintly pastor
of Ars inspires the spiritual renewal of the priest as a humble and trusting co-worker of the Bishops in communion
with the Roman Pontiff, building up the Church in unity
and love.

Contemplating the saintly life of Saint John Mary Vianney, Father Miller rightly devotes a particular reflection to
the Sacrament of Penance or Reconciliation. When Father

Vianney was sent to Ars, he was told that there was "little love of God" in the parish and that it was his mission to bring the love of God to the parish. The reason that there was little love of God was the failure of the faithful to confess their sins regularly and to receive God's merciful forgiveness. When one knows the love of God, even in an initial way, he discovers his own distance from God, his sinfulness, and desires to draw near to God through the confession and absolution of his sins.

Saint John Mary Vianney took up his particularly challenging mission by teaching the faithful about sin and the forgiveness of sins in the Sacrament of Penance and by devoting himself to hours of prayer before the Blessed Sacrament, during which he was available to the faithful to hear their confessions and to give them absolution. Father Miller explains: "As representing Christ and the Church, the Curé of Ars understood that his mission was to complete the work of grace by *re-presenting* the sacrifice of the cross first, for the forgiveness of sins in confession, and then, in the Eucharistic sacrifice." As Pope Benedict XVI has observed in the letter by which he proclaimed the Year for Priests, the crisis of the Sacrament of Penance, which priests face in our time, is similar to the crisis which Saint John Vianney faced. He urges the priest never to be content with the failure of the faithful to have access to the Sacrament but to follow the example of the saintly pastor of Ars who "sought in every way, by his preaching and his powers of persuasion, to help his parishioners to rediscover the meaning and beauty of the sacrament of Penance, presenting it as an inherent demand of the Eucharistic presence".[4]

---

[4] Pope Benedict XVI, *Letter Proclaiming a Year for Priests*, no. 8.

Fittingly, a special reflection is reserved for the relationship of the priest to the Blessed Virgin Mary, the relationship so richly exemplified in the priestly life of Saint John Mary
Vianney. Even as the Mother of God stood with Saint John
the Evangelist at the foot of the Cross, even so she accompanies every priest, from the first moment of the call to the
priesthood, as his spiritual mother, comforting and sustain-
ing him. For the Curé of Ars and for every priest, the holy
bond or "Sacred Alliance" of the Blessed Virgin Mary and
the priest is understood, in particular, in the light of the mystery of the Immaculate Conception. Even as Mary was preserved from all stain of original or actual sin from the moment
of her conception, so that she could be the fitting vessel of
the coming of divine grace into the world, so she is, in a
special way, the instrument of the grace of the priestly vocation and mission by which divine grace reaches many souls.
In the words of Father Miller, it "is not Mary's mission to
preach the Gospel, or administer the sacraments, or govern
the Church" but "to *accompany* those who share in the mission of her Son as priests and make their work fruitful through
her motherly intercession in heaven".

The final reflection invites us to leave Ars for a few hours
to make a related pilgrimage to nearby Paray-le-Monial, a place
made holy by the apparitions of the Sacred Heart of Jesus to
Saint Margaret Mary in the years 1673–1674. In pilgrimage
to Paray-le-Monial, a privileged place of the revelation of the
immeasurable and unceasing love of God toward us in the glorious pierced Heart of Jesus, the pilgrimage to Ars reaches a
new fullness, a completion, in the deeper understanding of
"the love of the Heart of Jesus," which is the priesthood. In
the words of Father Miller: "The *Grace of Ars* manifests itself
with a mystical fullness in Paray-le-Monial." At the sanctuary of the Sacred Heart of Jesus, we see, in a new light, Saint

John Vianney as the "icon of the Divine Bridegroom of the Church".

In urging the reader to go on pilgrimage to Ars, Father Miller reassures us: "In that small, out-of-the-way place that has been so profoundly touched by God, there is hardly a thing to do except pray and only one person to get to know!" Going on pilgrimage to Ars, physically or mystically, one gets to know Jesus Christ our Priest in his faithful brother, Saint John Mary Vianney, especially through prayer and the reception of the Sacraments of Penance and the Holy Eucharist. In that encounter, in the Sacred Heart of Jesus, is the fount of the "interior renewal" of priests "for the sake of a stronger and more incisive witness to the Gospel in today's world".[5] At Ars, in a most special way, priests can respond to the loving call of our Holy Father: "Dear priests, Christ is counting on you. In the footsteps of the Curé of Ars, let yourselves be enthralled by him."[6]

It is a source of great joy for me to commend to your reading *The Grace of Ars*. It is my prayer that it will be for many priests an apt instrument of our "interior renewal" for the care of souls in our time and that it will inspire in all readers a deeper knowledge and love of the "immense gift which priests represent, not only for the Church, but also for humanity itself".[7]

The Most Reverend Raymond Leo Burke
Archbishop Emeritus of Saint Louis
Prefect of the Supreme Tribunal of the Apostolic Signatura
August 29, 2009—Feast of the Beheading of Saint John the Baptist

---

[5] Ibid., no. 1.
[6] Ibid., no. 16.
[7] Ibid., no. 1.

I

The Pilgrimage to Ars

Early Easter Sunday morning, 2004, three priests, fifteen seminarians, and I left the Pontifical North American College in Rome for a retreat in Ars, France. The three priests, in the process of completing their graduate studies in Rome, were approaching their first anniversary of ordination. For some of the men, this was to be their retreat for either the priesthood or the diaconate. For the younger seminarians, it was an opportunity to spend some time in prayer. For me, the retreat master, it was an adventure—my first journey outside of the college after some physical health difficulties. The thought of the trip and the retreat in unfamiliar surroundings was daunting to me, but I was determined to go. For each of us, the journey to Ars was a pilgrimage that brought many personal graces and insights into the nature of the priesthood.

Throughout the three decades of my priesthood, I had rarely felt drawn to the Curé of Ars. I thought his images made him appear severe, eccentric, and unapproachable, even though I was aware that literally hundreds of thousands of men and women approached him during his lifetime to receive God's forgiveness in the sacrament of penance. Although I admired his asceticism, his devotion to prayer, his zeal for the sacraments, and his many charismatic gifts, I had difficulty connecting with him on a personal level. I did not exactly dismiss him as a priest from a different time and culture, but I was tempted to do so. I must also admit that I never was comfortable with this mind-set, especially since the priests I admire most are devoted to Saint John Vianney.

That Easter night, after twelve years of work in seminaries and more than twelve hours in a van, we caught sight of the basilica that enshrines the mortal remains of Saint John Vianney. As we drove past the shrine on our way to the seminary, the site of the retreat, I had the sense that the Curé had called us to this small, out-of-the-way village in France to reveal those facets of the priesthood that transcend all times and every culture. As we entered the parish of the Curé of Ars, I felt the responsibility of facilitating a spiritual encounter of eighteen young men with the patron saint of parish priests. By the end of the first day of the retreat, this concern vanished. I realized that the place, and the saint of the place, had already captured us spiritually. John Vianney was the retreat master.

Each day, we gathered at the basilica to celebrate the Holy Eucharist at the altar where Saint John Vianney is buried. The retreatants spent a great amount of time each day in personal prayer at the basilica. We also had our own private chapel in the seminary for Morning Prayer and Evening Prayer as well as adoration of the Blessed Sacrament.

I had prepared a booklet for spiritual reading that contained papal teaching on the Curé of Ars as the model of the diocesan priesthood, works well worth pondering, including Blessed Pope John XXIII's encyclical *From the Beginning of Our Priesthood* and Pope John Paul II's Letter to Priests for Holy Thursday of 1986. Because we had planned to end the retreat with Mass at Paray-le-Monial, the site of the apparition of the Sacred Heart of Jesus, I included Pope

Pius XII's encyclical on the Sacred Heart, *Haurietis Aquas*, in the collection. Near the midpoint of the retreat, the Benedictine sisters who staff the sanctuary invited us to view a fine video on the life and work of the Curé of Ars. During lunch and dinner, we took turns reading from a popular short biography of the Curé of Ars.[1]

Although I presented two conferences a day on the priesthood,[2] it became evident that pondering the saint's life in Ars, especially in his own parish church, was the substance of the retreat. In fact, concrete objects in the church— namely, the pulpit, the saint's catechetical desk, the shrine dedicated to our Blessed Mother, and, in a special way, the confessional—became rays of light revealing the depths of the ministerial priesthood. The more time we spent in the small church, the more each of these objects pointed directly toward the altar of sacrifice.

Without a doubt, the center of the Curé's life was the daily celebration of the Holy Eucharist. At the altar, John Vianney made the Calvary sacrifice of Christ sacramentally present and united his own life and sacrifices and his people's to his Lord's. In receiving Christ's Body and Blood in Holy Communion, the priest opened himself to daily transformation in Christ, the High Priest.

The saint returned to the altar of sacrifice several times a day to pray the *Liturgy of the Hours*. He appreciated that the

---

[1] Bartholomew O'Brien, *The Curé of Ars: Patron Saint of Parish Priests* (Charlotte, N.C.: TAN Books, 1987).

[2] My major sources on Saint John Vianney are the papal teaching listed above, his own sermons and catechism lessons, and the standard (and, I might add, excellent) biography entitled *The Curé d'Ars: Saint Jean-Marie-Baptiste Vianney* by the Abbé François (Francis) Trochu, trans. Dom Ernest Graf, O.S.B. (London: Burns, Oates and Washbourne, 1927; reprint Rockford, Ill.: TAN Books, 1977). This biography is, in my opinion, on the "must-read" list for all priests and seminarians.

divine office both extended the praise of the Eucharist throughout the day and presented other opportunities to unite himself to Christ in intercessory prayer for the Church and, in particular, for his people.

At the center of John Vianney's consciousness was the certainty that Christ had called him to the priesthood to celebrate the Eucharist and to integrate all other activity into that paramount act of worship. If the character of holy orders is indeed the charism of Jesus, the Good Shepherd, it is supernaturally natural for the priest to discover deep springs of pastoral charity in his heart. This supernatural instinct impelled John Vianney to go and seek out his people when he took up his post in Ars.

In February 1818, the vicar general of Father Vianney's diocese appointed him to Ars, saying, "There is not much love of God in that parish. It is your mission to instill it there." The faith of the people had been deeply wounded by the French Revolution. Father Vianney knew he had to bring healing and reconciliation to a shattered flock. He immediately began to pray and fast for his people and to practice other forms of corporeal penance as well. He was always available to his parishioners, embracing each as a member of his family. The people took notice of his authenticity as a priest, his zeal for the Eucharist, his long hours of prayer in front of the tabernacle in the parish church, and his concern for their salvation. Feeling that he loved them as a father, they were drawn to him.

Each Sunday, he mounted the pulpit in his humble parish church and called the people to faith and conversion. Although he fearlessly confronted sinful behavior, challenging his people to change, the pulsating central motif of his sermons was the merciful love of the Heart of Jesus present in the Eucharist.

Likewise, he took his responsibility as catechist seriously. He instructed the young *daily*, carefully preparing them to receive the sacraments of penance, confirmation, and the Holy Eucharist. Understanding that the adult parishioners likewise needed catechesis, Saint John Vianney did not hesitate to provide practical instruction whenever he spoke to them. He did not relinquish this duty even during the years when many people came each day for confession. When he catechized as an old, worn-out priest, most people could neither hear nor understand him, but they wept at the sight of the faithful minister of the Word of God. They sensed in faith that Christ was preaching his gospel from the pulpit in Ars through this simple parish priest.

Neither Scripture or dogma, on the one hand, nor homiletics or catechetics, on the other, were in conflict in his priestly mind and heart. He understood the organic and indispensable relationship of one to the other. He grasped in faith and with the aid of the gifts of the Holy Spirit how each of these realities is intimately related to confession and the Holy Eucharist.

In his work of door-to-door evangelization, in his catechetical ministry, and in his liturgical preaching, John Vianney encouraged his parishioners to avail themselves of Christ's mercy in the sacrament of penance. Slowly, the people began to come, and they never stopped: first the parishioners, then folk from neighboring parishes, then people from all over France—and beyond. Word began to spread: "There is a priest in Ars who understands everything, who reads hearts, who heals broken lives, who restores peace with God." It is estimated that in the last decade of his life, over eighty thousand people sought him out for confession each year. He sat in his uncomfortable confessional for fourteen or more hours a day, often hearing over two hundred confessions. People waited for days for a few minutes of his time.

It would be an egregious omission not to include mention of the shrine to Our Lady erected by the Curé of Ars. The priest attributed all the good he did as a priest to her motherly intercession and gave her full credit for the spiritual success of his ministry in the confessional. In fact, it has been noted that great numbers of penitents began to come to Ars after the Curé had publicly consecrated his parish to Mary under the title of the Immaculate Conception. Then there is his tender friendship with the martyr Philomena, to whom he attributed all the miracles of nature and grace that God worked through him.

Standing near the parish church of Ars is the "Providence", built and supported by the saint—an orphanage and school for girls, just one facet of the many works of charity of the parish priest of Ars. The biography we read at table during the retreat informed us that the saint used the entire inheritance he had received from his father to build and furnish the orphanage. He also provided religious and secular education for all the children of his parish, visited the sick, regularly gave all he had to the poor—even his meager meals—and lived like a pauper himself in the parish house. The seminarians noted that the Curé of Ars had many theological books in his presbytery, evidence that, although he had struggled with his studies in the seminary, he never forgot the importance of studying the Word of God for the sake of pastoral effectiveness.

We ended the retreat by making the short journey to the beautiful mountain town of Paray-le-Monial. There we celebrated Mass in the chapel of the apparitions of the Sacred Heart of Jesus to Saint Margaret Mary Alacoque. I will say more about the relationship of Ars and Paray-le-Monial later.

Suffice it to say here that Saint John Vianney defined the priesthood in terms of Jesus' Sacred Heart: "The priest continues the work of redemption on earth.... If we really understood the priest on earth, we would die not of fright but of love.... The Priesthood is the love of the heart of Jesus."[3]

After the retreat, I had many occasions to reflect on the experience of Ars in my personal prayer and in discussions with the retreatants. Many observed that simply spending time in the parish church of Ars pruned back many nonessential elements of priestly life and forced them to consider the fundamental nature of the priesthood.

Impossible to miss were certain obvious lights and graces: the absolute certainty that the daily celebration of the Holy Eucharist must be the integrating core of priestly life and ministry; a new understanding of the relationship of evangelization, catechesis, liturgical preaching, and, in a privileged place, the sacrament of penance to the Holy Eucharist; the awareness that zeal for teaching the Catholic faith and administering the sacraments propels the priest gladly to embrace the gospel counsels of poverty, chastity, and obedience that, in turn, facilitate his service to the people; the intuitive certainty that the personal sanctity of the priest affects the disposition of the people in their reception of the Word of God and the sacraments; and the conviction that the priest must perform and organize the works of charity in his parish. There were other graces too personal to articulate that will perhaps be recognized only in time and as various charisms unfold in the lives of priests who, following the example of the Curé of Ars, are willing to give their all for Christ and his flock.

---

[3] *Catechism of the Catholic Church*, no. 1589.

There is something very tangible, very physical, about our recollections of the week in Ars: the altar, the pulpit, the catechetical desk, the confessional, the shrine to Our Lady, the orphanage and school, the memory of the simple man who lived day in and day out in this church, selflessly allowing the Holy Spirit to transform his parish and his world through his faithful service of the mystery of Christ.

We left Ars on the Sunday that completes the Octave of Easter, Divine Mercy Sunday, to make the trip back to Rome. I recall wondering on the way if and when I would return to Ars. I had my answer almost immediately. Students began to ask me to repeat the pilgrimage and retreat during Easter Week of the following year. The number of retreatants doubled in 2005.

Returning from Rome to the United States in June 2005, I was reassigned to Mount Saint Mary's Seminary in Emmitsburg, Maryland. The ordination class of 2007 heard about the retreat in Ars and asked if I might consider organizing a "Mount retreat" for them. With the help of a capable student and travel agent, twenty of us crossed the Atlantic during the spring break and made our way to Ars. That following summer, I accompanied a group of priests to the parish of the Curé of Ars and again led a retreat.

Then in 2009, yet another group of twenty students from Mount Saint Mary's Seminary asked for a retreat in Ars. As in the aftermath of the previous retreats, there were high spirits, reports of powerful and transforming graces, a new enthusiasm for a simple priestly lifestyle, and a desire to emulate the Curé of Ars in the practice of the evangelical counsels as a diocesan priest. Many of the men expressed one or both of the following convictions: "Finally, I discovered the image of the priest that I believe the Holy Spirit is calling me to embrace." "Now I understand why the priest is called Father." After having led five retreats in the parish of the Curé of Ars, I returned to the seminary more convinced than ever that there is a strong medicine in Ars to heal the ills of the priesthood in our times.

On March 16, 2009, a week or so after we returned to the seminary, Pope Benedict XVI announced the Year for Priests, which will highlight the life and ministry of the Curé of Ars. This special year of grace began on the Solemnity of the Sacred Heart of Jesus, June 19, 2009, and will end exactly one year later. It included the celebration of the 150th anniversary of the death of Saint John Vianney. As part of the festivities, the Holy Father will proclaim Saint John Vianney the patron of all priests and not just of parish priests.

As soon as the Mount seminarians read the press releases on the Year for Priests, they began to ask for a retreat in Ars during this year dedicated to priestly life and ministry. Several faculty members and priest alumni requested to be included on the list for the 2010 trip to Ars. I am convinced that the Year for Priests will attract more priests and seminarians to Ars than ever before.

My spiritual experiences in Ars as well as the remarkable initiative of our Holy Father in designating June 19, 2009, to June 19, 2010, the Year for Priests prompted me to publish the conferences that I had prepared over the years on the Curé of Ars. Reading over the text, I realize that this book is, strictly speaking, neither biography nor theology but, rather, a spiritual reflection based on the life and work of the Curé of Ars as seen through the lens of the theology of the priesthood, which I have the privilege to teach to future priests.

I encourage my brother priests, diocesan and religious alike, to make a pilgrimage to Ars during the Year for Priests or in the years ahead. If you are able to find an empty room in the seminary of Ars, by all means, stay there![4] You will be perfectly at home, and, as one of the seminarians put it, "You will find yourself in a holy and safe place."

If you are not able to make the pilgrimage to Ars, go in spirit. Hopefully, these reflections will help you make a spiritual journey to Ars, whenever and wherever you make your yearly retreat. The book is made up of ten chapters, suitable, I hope, for a five-day retreat or simply for spiritual reading. I hope that these reflections on the priesthood will help the lay faithful to appreciate more fully the gift of the ministerial priesthood and pray more fervently for the sanctification of their priests. I pray that these conferences will inspire a young man or two to hear the call of Christ and respond to it.

In a remarkable way, Pope Benedict XVI has empowered the Curé of Ars to minister to all the priests of the Church during the Year for Priests. With gratitude for the indefatigable zeal of these two priests of God, Pope Benedict XVI and Saint John Vianney, and remembering all the priests and seminarians with whom I have prayed in Ars throughout the years, let us go to Ars in spirit. In that small, out-of-the-way place that has been so profoundly touched by God, there is hardly a thing to do except pray and only one person to get to know!

---

[4] Contact information for the seminary of Ars:
   Foyer Sacerdotal Jean-Paul II
   352, Chemin de la Percellière
   01480 Ars sur Formans, France
   Telephone: (33) 04 74 08 19 00
   E-mail: fsacerdotal.ars@wanadoo.fr

2

The Call of Christ

The late Monsignor Eugene Kevane, once dean of the School of Education at Catholic University of America, devoted a number of lectures in his course "Jesus, the Divine Teacher" to the topic of New Testament discipleship. He explained that Our Lord began his public ministry by announcing the coming of the Kingdom of God and calling the people of Israel to believe in him and turn away from sin. Through this work of evangelization, the Lord gathered many disciples, men and women, who were attentive to his word, witnessed his many signs, and followed him from place to place for varied motives. Monsignor Kevane often noted that Jesus was, at first, perceived simply as a rabbi (teacher) by his disciples (students) and only progressively as the Divine Teacher.

The Evangelists tell us that in the midst of his proclamation of the Kingdom, Jesus was fully aware of the scope of the mission given to him. His Father willed that his word should be brought to every human person, not only in Israel but also in the whole world and until the end of time. Monsignor Kevane explained that Jesus deliberately chose twelve of his many disciples to share in a unique way in the mission that he had received from his Father. The Evangelist Matthew writes:

> Jesus went about all the cities and villages, teaching in their synagogues and preaching the gospel of the kingdom, and healing every disease and every infirmity. When he saw the crowds, he had compassion for them, because they were harassed and helpless, like sheep without a shepherd. Then he said to his disciples, "The harvest is plentiful, but the laborers are few; pray therefore the Lord of the harvest to send out laborers into his harvest." (Mt 9:35–37)

The Father in heaven, "the Lord of the harvest", immediately heard the prayer of Jesus and his disciples and answered it. Looking out at his many disciples, Jesus, instructed interiorly by the Father, "called to him his twelve disciples and gave them authority over unclean spirits, to cast them out, and to heal every disease and every infirmity" (Mt 10:1).

He conferred his authority on them, giving them power and sending them out to announce the coming of the Kingdom of God. Throughout the rest of his public ministry, the Twelve remained close to Jesus. They traveled with the Lord and lived with him.

Monsignor Kevane taught that Christ, in the traditional Hebraic manner, formed his own rabbinical school. Like today, students of Jesus' day chose their own school. This means simply that they chose a rabbi to study under. But in Jesus' rabbinical school, there was one major difference: The rabbi chose his disciples. "You did not choose me, but I chose you" (Jn 15:16). Christ was preparing them to take up his teaching and become teachers in their own right with his authority. Christ was forming the apostles to continue his mission as shepherd of his disciples after his death and Resurrection.

There are several significant facts to notice and keep in mind.

First, the apostles were chosen to share in Christ's life and mission, to be his envoys. They must *be* with him, and only then will they be sent out. Priestly ontology both precedes and governs priestly function. In other words, the apostles, through spiritual intimacy with Christ, would be given the capacity to do the things that he did. This transformation means nothing less than an abiding and real presence of Christ in his apostles.

Second, the apostles were chosen out of a larger number of disciples to shepherd all disciples in the Person of Christ, the head and bridegroom of the Church. The number twelve bespeaks the creation of a new Israel, a new people of God. These are the foundation stones of this new people. Their transmission of the teaching of Christ will ever be normative in the life of the Church. Believers in every time and place will come to Christ through their preaching, which, through the inspiration of the Holy Spirit, is found in the Christian Scriptures. Their interpretation of the Scriptures and all that makes up the Christian way of life will also always remain at the heart of the Church through the indwelling presence of the Spirit. Christ will govern the Church in this world until the end of time through the men who succeed the apostles as bishops.

Third, although the apostles are called into being as a body, a college, and will ever remain such, each is called by name. Peter's name is changed to underscore his unique role among the others. John is the "beloved disciple". Unity of faith does not rule out individuality and personality. Herein is the foundation of the Church's understanding of vocation.[1]

---

[1] Although it is necessary to hold in faith that the bishops succeed the apostles and share in the fullness of the ministerial priesthood, nevertheless, presbyters, by their consecration and mission as co-workers of the order of bishops, share in the apostolic mission at the *second rank* of the priesthood.

Fourth, Christ chose seventy-two disciples to participate in his mission and that of the twelve apostles (Lk 10:1–20). At the time of Christ, the Hebrews believed that there were seventy-two peoples on the face of the earth. The number seventy-two, then, signifies the universality of the new people of God founded by Christ. The Lord gave the seventy-two disciples a mission similar to the mission entrusted to the apostles. They were to announce the coming of the Kingdom of God and call all to faith in Christ and to conversion from sin. Because they had been sent forth by Christ, the seventy-two disciples, like the apostles, had authority to cast out evil spirits to prepare the way for the Kingdom of God.

A simple perusal of the Gospels indicates that Jesus intended to give the twelve apostles a participation in his power and authority. First, there is the vocation, the call: "Come, follow me!" Then the special time to *be with* Jesus began. During this period, which began on the day of their call and reached fullness only with the outpouring of the Holy Spirit on Pentecost, Jesus accomplished the consecration of the twelve apostles, which caused them to participate ontologically in his mission and his holiness.[2]

---

[2] In the seventeenth chapter of Saint John's Gospel, we find the prayer of consecration Jesus prayed over the Twelve on the night before he died. For centuries, this chapter has been called Jesus' "High Priestly Prayer". Therein Christ offered himself as a sacrifice for the salvation of the world. He also set the Twelve apart, consecrating them to share in the mission he had received from his Father: "Sanctify them in the truth; your word is truth. As you sent me into the world, so I have sent them into the world. And for their sake I consecrate myself, that they also may be consecrated in truth" (Jn 17:17–19). . . .

Jesus then prayed for all those who would benefit from their ministry throughout the ages: "I do not pray for these only [the Twelve], but also for those who believe in me through their word, that they may all be one; even as you, Father, are in me, and I in you, that they also may be in us, so that the world may believe that you have sent me" (Jn 17:20–21).

In this consecration, the Son of God conferred on the apostles and their successors the authority to carry out the mission of evangelization for the whole world (Mk 16:15–20). He gave them universal jurisdiction to preach the Gospel everywhere in order to call the Church into being and govern her with his authority (Mt 22:18–20); the capacity to celebrate the Eucharist and to communicate that capacity to others (Lk 22:19–20); and the authority and power to forgive sins (Jn 20:19–23). Christ conferred a unique primacy on Peter, making him and his successors the special sign and instrument of the unity of the apostolic college and the universal Church.

The New Testament is unambiguous in affirming that the apostles had authority from Christ to join other men to their mission.[3] As they awaited the coming of the Holy

---

[3] The Fathers of the Second Vatican Council, in the Dogmatic Constitution on the Church *Lumen Gentium* (20), explain that the bishops take the place of the Twelve "by divine institution": "That divine mission that was committed by Christ to the apostles is destined to last until the end of the world.... In fact, not only had they various helpers in their ministry, but, in order that the mission entrusted to them might be continued after their death, they consigned, by will and testament, as it were, to their immediate collaborators the duty of completing and consolidating the work they had begun, urging them to tend to the whole flock, in which the Holy Spirit had appointed them to shepherd the Church of God (cf. Acts 20:28). They accordingly designated such men and then made the ruling that likewise on their death other proven men should take over their ministry. Amongst those various offices which have been exercised in the Church from the earliest times the chief place, according to the witness of tradition, is held by the function of those who, through their appointment to the dignity and responsibility of bishop, and in virtue consequently of the unbroken succession, going back to the beginning, are regarded as transmitters of the apostolic line.... In that way, then, with priests and deacons as helpers, the bishops received the charge of the community, presiding in God's stead over the flock, of which they are the shepherds in that they are teachers of doctrine, ministers of sacred worship, and holders of office in government.... This sacred synod consequently teaches that the bishops have by divine institution taken the place of

Spirit, the eleven apostles chose Matthias to take Judas' place. On Pentecost, the apostles began to exercise their authority and power in the Person of Christ, the head of the Church (*in persona Christi capitis ecclesiae*). They preached with his authority, presided over the breaking of the bread, and began to structure the growing Christian community. Just as the twelve apostles were called from the body of disciples, so they called others from that same body to share in their apostolic ministry—for instance, Saul and Barnabas, Silas, Timothy and Titus, and the seven deacons of Acts 6. They passed on their authority and power through the laying on of hands (see 1 Tim 4:14 and 2 Tim 1:6).[4]

Priests (presbyters) are co-workers of the order of bishops and share in the apostolic ministry in the second rank of the priesthood. In a sense, they succeed the seventy-two disciples of the gospel who had been given a mission similar to that of the twelve apostles. Like the bishops who

---

the apostles as pastors of the Church, in such wise that whoever listens to them is listening to Christ and whoever despises them despises Christ and him who sent Christ" (Lk 10:16).

[4] Our Holy Father Pope Benedict has on several occasions used two passages, one from the Acts of the Apostles and the other from the First Letter of Peter, to demonstrate the phenomenon of apostolic succession in the New Testament. In Acts 20, Saint Paul, speaking to the presbyters of the church of Ephesus, writes, "Take heed to yourselves and to all the flock, in which the Holy Spirit has made you guardians [bishops], to feed the Church of the Lord which he obtained with his own blood" (Acts 20:28).

Similarly, in his First Letter, Saint Peter identifies himself with presbyters who are leading the Church of God in Rome: "So I exhort the elders among you, as a fellow elder [presbyter] and a witness of the sufferings of Christ as well as a partaker in the glory that is to be revealed. Tend the flock of God that is your charge, exercising the oversight ["bishoping"], not by constraint but willingly, not for shameful gain but eagerly, not as domineering over those in your charge but being examples to the flock. And when the chief Shepherd is manifested you will obtain the unfading crown of glory" (1 Pet 5:1–4).

succeed the apostles in the fullness of the priesthood, priests are called personally by Christ to follow him in his priestly ministry. They are asked to spend an extended time with him in prayer and study before they are sent out on mission. They are set apart and made holy, that is, consecrated to the service of Christ and the Church through the laying on of hands and the prayer of consecration in presbyteral ordination. They are sealed by the Holy Spirit with a new character, a spiritual and indelible reality inhering in the soul that configures them to Christ the Priest and empowers them to act in his Person, especially in the celebration of the Eucharistic Sacrifice. In communion with the college of bishops and under the fatherly guidance of a local bishop, the priest receives authority and power from the Lord in ordination to preach the Word of God, administer the sacraments, and shepherd a portion of the flock of Christ.

Since the foundation of the Church, Christ has called men in every place and generation to share in his priesthood. Obviously, each man is called to serve at a particular moment of human history and to face the various crises of the secular and ecclesiastical culture of that time.

In every age and crisis of culture, Christ calls men to the priesthood. Jesus called the twelve apostles during the years of his public ministry, when Rome dominated all of Palestine with a strong and ruthless arm. He asked them to follow him when the people of Israel were desperately divided and confused over the mission of the promised messiah and the kind of salvation he would bring to Israel.

He called John Vianney to service in a Church that had been decimated by bloody martyrdom and was still experiencing the vertigo of enlightenment thought and the violent resurgence of pagan immorality. In the twenty-first century, he calls men to preach his gospel to people immersed in a humanistic, hedonistic culture that worships the god of relativism. He invites them to be his mediators in a Church that has been scarred by decades of theological dissent, liturgical and sacramental abuse, confusion over the roles of priests and laypeople in the Church, clerical sexual scandals, and weak leadership.

The apostles accepted the challenge and brought the ancient pagan world to the feet of Christ. John Vianney responded and brought hundreds of thousands of people to a little backwater village in France to experience the mercy of Christ in confession. What might a wholehearted response to the call of Christ accomplish in the world today?

Jean-Marie-Baptiste (John) Vianney was born on May 8, 1786, in the village of Dardilly, a parish of the ancient local Church of Lyon. The son of a farmer, he grew up during the years of the French Revolution. The charity his parents showed to the sick, the poor, and the homeless impressed itself indelibly on John. He was also marked by his family's spirit of prayer and devotion to the Blessed Virgin and the saints. Although he had heard the call of the Lord early in life, he confided his vocation to his mother at the age of seventeen, in the immediate aftermath of the French Revolution. At first, his father, reluctant to lose a reliable worker on his farm, opposed the young man's entry into the seminary.

The young Vianney experienced a Church in crisis. In fact, the Catholic Church was brutally suppressed by the revolutionaries and replaced by the national church of their own creation. This national church was an ecclesial body that had been compromised almost beyond recognition. Many of the French bishops and priests, to save their lives and property, had betrayed the Church of their baptism by renouncing any real communion with the Holy See and accepting dogmas of the Revolution that were hostile to the gospel of Christ. John Vianney, thanks to his family, had absolutely no personal contact with this schismatic church.

It was his older sister, Catherine, who first sensed danger when their faithful pastor was replaced by a "juror priest", that is, one who had taken the oath of loyalty to the revolutionary government. Abbé François Trochu in *The Curé d'Ars* explains how John Vianney's twelve-year-old sister sensed a serious problem in the new pastor:

> In the pulpit the new pastor did not speak quite like M. Rey, nor on the same topics. His sermons were interlarded with the words *citizen, civism,* and *constitution*. He so far forgot himself as to criticize his predecessors. The congregation was more promiscuous and scantier than of yore; persons who were noted for their fervour were no longer seen in church—where did they go to Mass on Sundays?—others on the contrary were there and occupied the best seats, who previously had hardly ever darkened the threshold of the sacred edifice. Catherine felt anxious and she confided her secret fears to her mother.[5]

As soon as Matthieu and Marie Vianney came to understand the state of the Church in France, they withdrew from their parish church and sought out those priests who had refused to sign the oath and were being hunted down by the constitutional government. Consequently, John Vianney from the age of five was raised in an underground Catholic Church. The heroic fidelity of his parents, extended family, and neighbors formed Vianney's understanding of both Church and priesthood. John Vianney's parents risked losing their property and their lives by harboring priests who refused to betray the Church in her moment of crisis.

[5] Abbé Francis Trochu, *The Curé d'Ars: Saint Jean-Marie-Baptiste Vianney*, trans. Dom Ernest Graf, O.S.B. (Rockford, Ill.: TAN Books, 1977), p. 12.

The family attended Mass in barns or private homes in the shadows of evening whenever there was an opportunity.

As a boy, except for the very brief exposure to the juror priest, John experienced only those priests, religious, and faithful whose lives had been endangered because of their loyalty to the Church. As a consequence, he was unable to remember the Church of his childhood without thinking of the persecution. In nearby Lyon, only miles from his home, over twenty thousand loyal Catholics were executed for their faith in the course of a year. Authors claim that it is miraculous that the Vianney family escaped the Revolution with their lives. Without the slightest trace or ambiguity or compromise, they rejected the constitutional church and remained faithful to the Catholic Church.

John Vianney received his first Holy Communion in a barn at the age of thirteen with sixteen other children. Farmers who were stationed outside baled hay in an effort to distract attention from the clandestine ceremony within. The Church of Vianney's youth had the vitality and stamina of the Church of the Roman catacombs, a Church pure, holy, and conformed to Christ crucified. He experienced priests who had the courage and generosity of the apostles and the first Christian martyrs. In the midst of this difficult yet exhilarating situation, John Vianney heard the call of Jesus to follow him as a priest.

After the ascendancy of Napoleon Bonaparte, some degree of normalcy was restored to the Church in France. A concordat was signed by the French government and the Holy See and became law in 1802. Although there would be many significant disturbances in the years to come, the schismatic church had seen its day. In this new atmosphere, John Vianney, who had long sensed a call to the priesthood, was now free to begin his seminary studies.

The young man suffered from several disadvantages: Because of the turmoil in the society of his childhood, John Vianney began his formal education around the age of eight or nine and never really caught up intellectually with his peers. Latin was all but impossible for him. Father Charles Balley, a parish priest, sensing the young man's goodness and sanctity, offered to be his tutor. After making a pilgrimage to the shrine of Saint Francis Regis, Vianney found the inner resources he needed to pursue the study of Latin and other rudimentary subjects in preparation for his philosophical and theological studies. His goodwill and his holiness were never lacking. Although he seems to have had a limited capacity for abstract thought, Vianney was prepared spiritually and intellectually for the seminary by the heroically patient Father Balley.

At this time, an official in the diocesan curia forgot to put John Vianney's name on the official list of ecclesiastical students who were legally excluded from military conscription. Consequently, Vianney was drafted into Napoleon's army in 1809. Because of illness and personal ineptitude, he lagged behind the troops and found himself, by accident, a deserter. He lived in hiding with an assumed identity for nearly two years among devout Catholics who were far from sympathetic toward Napoleon's military campaigns. Living with the constant threat of arrest and imprisonment, Vianney showed signs of a highly developed life of prayer and an apostolic spirit.

Having received amnesty for his desertion from the military, Vianney returned to Father Balley's rectory to continue his classical studies and prepare to enter the minor seminary in 1812. During his one year of philosophical studies, Vianney struggled with academics for a variety of reasons. Some of the seminary professors had been influenced by the philosophy of the enlightenment and promoted the thought of René Descartes. Vianney, by modern standards a late vocation, sensed something askew in the professors' approach to philosophy but could not articulate the difficulty. For this and other reasons, chief among them his inability to master Latin, Vianney finished the academic year with the grade of "very weak" in general knowledge.

The following year, 1813, John Vianney entered the major seminary of Saint Irenaeus in Lyon. After six months, he was asked to leave the seminary because the faculty decided that he could not learn the theology necessary for priestly ordination. After an initial bout of discouragement that included a temptation to join a congregation of teaching brothers, Vianney returned again to Father Balley's rectory. The faithful friend and spiritual guide of the young man now tutored him in Catholic doctrine, morality, liturgy, and canon law.

Father Balley was convinced of two things: Christ had called John Vianney to the priesthood, and once ordained, he would do great things for the Church. Balley, himself a holy and zealous man, was not ready to give up.

At the end of that academic year, with the encouragement of Father Balley, Vianney presented himself with his former seminary classmates before the canonical examiners for the preordination theological examination. As might be expected, Vianney failed the examination. The examiners suggested that he seek ordination in another diocese. Still convinced that Christ was calling Vianney to the priesthood, Father Balley challenged the verdict of the diocesan officials. With greater vigor, he continued his tutoring. As a result of the extended absence of the cardinal of Lyon from the archdiocese, Balley arranged for a private examination of the candidate by the vicar general, M. Courbon, who was known for his kindness and leniency. After the examination, in the rectory of Ecully, the vicar general gave his decision: John Vianney was "a model of holiness.... I summon him to come up for ordination [to the subdiaconate]. The grace of God will do the rest." [6] Likely, these are the most prophetic words ever spoken by the benevolent vicar general of Lyon!

Imagine John Vianney's joy! Jesus had called him years before to the priesthood. There was a pure and unfaltering assent in his heart to his vocation. The obstacles had been daunting and unrelenting, to say the least: first, the horrors of the French Revolution and the bloody persecution of the Church, during which only the force of Providence allowed the Vianney family to escape martyrdom; then, the Napoleonic Wars and the issue of desertion from military inscription, the experience of living for two years as a criminal with an assumed identity among strangers, the inability to learn Latin and the suffering caused by a possible learning disability, the discovery of unsound enlightenment thought in the minor seminary, dismissal from the major seminary after a short six-month stay, and finally, the failure of the canonical examination for holy orders and the suggestion that he take himself and his vocation to another diocese. In the midst of this proverbial train wreck, John Vianney received the ecclesial authentication of the call of Jesus from the vicar general of the archbishop of Lyon.

It is beneficial for the priest to remember the call of Christ in his life, to listen again to Jesus' strong, steady voice saying, "Come, follow me, and I will make you fishers of men". It is a consolation to revisit those first impulses to respond to the call of Christ.

[6] Ibid., p. 85.

The priest does well to think about the loved ones and friends who helped him say yes to Our Lord. Likely, there was a priest who offered encouragement. Surely there was the presence of the Blessed Mother. All grace, and in particular the grace of the priestly vocation, comes through her intercession and powerful maternal concern for the Church. The priest might call to mind too the opposition posed, perhaps by family members or friends, and the conflicts he encountered in his heart in the face of Christ's request to give him everything.

The priest should remember how helpless he felt and perhaps still feels as he considers the iron wall of secular humanism and relativism that every priest faces in our American culture. He may also have experienced a kind of persecution within the Church because of his fidelity to the gospel preached by Pope Paul VI, Pope John Paul II, and Pope Benedict XVI. Perhaps he intuits an encroaching persecution of the Church from without led by those who adhere to the principles of the culture of death. The trials of the contemporary Church are not exactly those that Saint John Vianney experienced, but there are disturbing similarities.

Listen to Jesus' words to his followers: "Unless you pick up your cross and follow in my footsteps, you cannot be my disciples." The priest might marvel at the graces he received to overcome trials and obstacles. Every priest and seminarian, if he is at all perceptive, has surely seen the movement of God in his life and experienced the Lord's saving power. It is ungrateful not to remember. A question to ponder in prayer: How was and is God working through these personal trials to form me into his priest specifically for this particular moment in the life of the Church in the United States of America?

Many priests and seminarians are uncomfortable with the contemporary image of the diocesan priest as an upper-middle-class single professional. John Vianney has the remedy for this unhappy image that has developed over the past several decades. The image of the priest presented by the Curé of Ars, hardly new, may indeed seem novel, challenging, and invigorating. In encountering John Vianney, the priest recognizes fully, or perhaps for the first time, the life to which Jesus has called him as a servant of the gospel.

There are priests who, through no fault of their own, received an unsound presentation of Catholic teaching during their seminary years and little or no spiritual formation. This malformation, a grave injustice to both priest and people, has surely affected and impoverished many souls. A pilgrimage to Ars presents an opportunity to repent, if repentance is in order, for not teaching the faith in its fullness and, in particular, for not presenting the Church's teaching on marital chastity, for the abuse of the sacraments of reconciliation and the Holy Eucharist, for a materialistic way of life, for clerical ambition, and for violations of the promises of obedience and priestly celibacy.

The pilgrimage also offers the opportunity to pray for and forgive those formators and mentors who, perhaps convinced that they were doing the right thing, withheld or distorted Catholic teaching and practice by their teaching and example. The pilgrimage to Ars is, in a way, the admission that no man is equal to the dignity of the priesthood and desperately needs the grace of Christ, the great High Priest. The pilgrimage offers the opportunity of a new beginning for all priests. During the Year for Priests, the Curé of Ars will do what he does best: He will help priests examine their consciences and make a humble confession of their sins, past and present, for the renewal of the priesthood.

In his pastoral visit to Paris in 1980, Pope John Paul II held Saint John Vianney up as the model priest formed according to the heart of Christ. Lamenting that he could not visit Ars, he said: "How much I would have liked to go as a pilgrim to Ars, if that had been possible! The Curé of Ars remains, in fact, for all countries, a peerless model both of the accomplishment of the ministry, and of the holiness of the minister, dedicated to prayer and penitence for the conversion of souls." [7]

"A peerless model"! These are powerful words that focus our full attention on the parish priest of Ars.

[7] "Address to the Clergy of Paris", May 30, 1980, in *L'Osservatore Romano*, Eng. ed., June 9, 1980, p. 4.

3

Consecration to Christ: Priestly Ordination

On the night before he died, Jesus Christ consecrated the twelve apostles priests of the new covenant. He had called them several years before; they had lived with him; he formed them through his teaching and his example. He had sent them out on mission to announce the coming of the Kingdom of God to the people of Israel and call them to faith and repentance. On Holy Thursday, Christ immersed the apostles in his personal holiness in a new way, creating in them the capacity to change bread and wine into his Body and Blood and make present the sacrifice of the Cross.

In the prayer of Christ found in the seventeenth chapter of Saint John's Gospel, the priest discovers his identity as minister of Christ, the great High Priest:

When Jesus had spoken these words, he lifted up his eyes to heaven and said, "Father, the hour has come; glorify your Son that the Son may glorify you, since you have given him power over all flesh, to give eternal life to all whom you have given him. And this is eternal life, that they know you the only true God, and Jesus Christ whom you have sent. I glorified you on earth, having accomplished the work which you gave me to do; and now,

Father, glorify me in your own presence with the glory which I had with you before the world was made.

"I have manifested your name to the men whom you gave me out of the world; they were yours, and you gave them to me, and they have kept your word. Now they know that everything that you have given me is from you; for I have given them the words which you gave me, and they have received them and know in truth that I came from you; and they have believed that you sent me. I am praying for them; I am not praying for the world but for those whom you have given me, for they are yours; all mine are yours, and yours are mine, and I am glorified in them. And now I am no more in the world, but they are in the world, and I am coming to you. Hoy Father, keep them in your name, which you have given me, that they may be one, even as we are one. While I was with them, I kept them in your name, which you have given me; I have guarded them, and none of them is lost but the son of perdition, that the Scripture might be fulfilled. But now I am coming to you; and these things I speak in the world, that they may have my joy fulfilled in themselves. I have given them your word; and the world has hated them because they are not of the world, even as I am not of the world. I do not pray that you should take them out of the world, but that you should keep them from the evil one. They are not of the world, even as I am not of the world. Sanctify them in the truth; your word is truth. As you sent me into the world, so I have sent them into the world. And for their sake I consecrate myself, that they also may be consecrated in truth.

"I do not pray for these only, but also for those who believe in me through their word, that they may all be one; even as you, Father, are in me, and I in you, that they also may be in us, so that the world may believe that you have sent me. The glory which you have given me I have given to them, that they may be one even as we are one, I in them and you in me, that they may become perfectly one, so that the world may know that you have sent me and have loved them even as you have loved me. Father, I desire that they also, whom you have given me, may be with me where I am, to behold my glory which you have given me in your love for me before the foundation of the world. O righteous Father, the world has not known you, but I have known you; and these know that you have sent me. I made known to them your name, and I will make it known, that the love with which you have loved me may be in them, and I in them." (Jn 17:1–26)

This prayer of Christ is the foundation of the prayer of consecration the bishop prays over him upon whom he has laid his hands in priestly ordination. Through the sacred sign of the imposition of hands that comes to us from the apostles and through the consecratory prayer, the risen Lord himself sets a man apart for priestly service and makes him holy.

During an ordination to the priesthood that I recently attended, a mystery became obvious to me that had escaped me, at least in some of its dimensions, in the past. I realized that the rite of ordination is a kind of Eucharist within the celebration of the Eucharist.

The ordination Mass begins as usual and continues through the Liturgy of the Word. Christ is present in the congregation gathered in his name. He is present in the bishop who presides and in the priests who concelebrate. He speaks to his people through the Word proclaimed and preached. He speaks especially to the men who are about to receive the gift of the priesthood.

Then, having promised to fulfill the duties of the priesthood, the candidates prostrate themselves in front of the altar. The congregation invokes the help of all the saints. At the end of the litany, the bishop offers the candidate to Christ for ordination. This is analogous to the presentation of the gifts in the celebration of the Holy Eucharist.

At Mass, the bishop or priest places the bread and wine on the altar, offering them to God, and asks Our Lord, through the Holy Spirit, to change them into his Body and Blood offered in sacrifice. In the rite of ordination, the bishop offers the candidates to God and asks him to confer on them the grace and power of the priesthood.

In silence, the bishop lays his hands on the head of each candidate. The laying on of hands is a great epiclesis, an invocation of the Holy Spirit. It is the same gesture the bishop and priests will make immediately before the consecration of the Eucharist, calling the Holy Spirit to come and transform the bread and wine into the Body and Blood of Christ. The bishop, performing this sacred sign that has been handed over to us by the apostles, calls the Holy Spirit to come and transform the candidate so that, participating in the holiness of Christ in a new way, he may act in the Person of Christ whenever he preaches the Word of God, administers the sacraments, and shepherds God's people. This solemn epiclesis continues, in a way, while all the presbyters in attendance lay their hands on the heads of the candidates, asking Christ to fill them with all the gifts and charisms of the Holy Spirit for their ministry.

Then the bishop, still acting in the Person of Christ, says the solemn prayer of consecration that brings the sacrament of holy orders to completion. Through this prayer and the laying on of hands, the Creator Spirit comes and seals the innermost being of the new priest with the spiritual and indelible sign of Christ, the great High Priest, transforming him at the core of his being. Speaking analogously in relation to the Eucharist, this prayer of consecration causes a kind of substantial change, not in the elements of bread and wine, but in a human person. It is not just a new function that is given to the priest. Theologians explain that the change effected by the sacrament of orders is ontological, in the order of being. The epiclesis and the consecration of holy orders make a man an *alter Christus*, another Christ, capable of acting in the Person of Christ, the head of the Church. At the heart of the transformation of holy orders is the character of the priesthood, that is, the sacred seal that internalizes in the priest the power to re-present (that is, make present) Christ's sacrifice in the Holy Mass and all the sacraments.

Saint Paul attests to the objective reality of this gift in both of his Letters to Timothy. The apostle reminds his spiritual son of the gift he received from God through the laying on of hands of the presbyters of the Church, a gift that remains permanently within him: "Do not neglect the gift you have, which was given you by prophetic utterance when the elders [presbyters] laid their hands on you" (1 Tim 4:14). Also, "I remind you to rekindle the gift of God that is within you through the laying on of my hands" (2 Tim 1:6).

This interior gift that Paul mentions is the indelible seal that sets the priest apart (*signum distinctivum*), configures him to Christ the High Priest (*signum configurativum*), excites in him the desire to be a living instrument of Jesus Christ (*signum dispositivum*), and obliges him to conform his life to Christ and the mystery of his Cross (*signum obligativum*). The character of holy orders is the inner sacrament that makes the priest a living sacrament, or sign, and instrument of Christ in the Church. It is this interior gift of the Spirit that creates in the new priest the capacity to change the substance of bread and wine into the sacred Body and Blood of Christ and to forgive sins.

The priestly vestments that are then given externalize the interior transformation that has taken place through the act of the Holy Trinity. The anointing of the priest's hands with chrism does the same. These rites are signs that the new priest has been set apart and made holy for the sake of service in the Church.

Then, as the bishop hands the new priest the bread and wine presented by the people of God, he urges him to model every facet of his life on the sacrifice he is about to offer to the Father: "Accept from the holy people of God the gifts to be offered to him. Know what you are doing, imitate the mystery you celebrate: model your life on the mystery of the Lord's cross."

After the sign of peace, the new priest performs his first priestly act: He joins the bishop and the other priests in offering the sacrifice of Christ to the Father for the salvation of all. As the new priest goes to the altar with the bishop, the ordination rite flows into the celebration of the Lord's sacrifice, which itself is the origin and source of the priesthood.

To witness the transforming effects of the sacrament of holy orders in a man, all one needs to do is look at the life of Saint John Marie Vianney. The twenty-nine-year-old man walked from the town of Ecully, not very far from Ars, to Grenoble to be ordained. It was a long walk in the summer heat, a distance of more than sixty miles. There he became a priest on August 13, 1815. No record indicates that any family members or friends were present at the ordination. The following morning, Vianney celebrated his first Mass with only a server. The triumphalism that sometimes characterizes ordinations and first Masses today was wholly absent.

It is plausible to think that God raised up John Vianney to make the character and grace of holy orders dramatically visible in the life of the Church. The saint of Ars shows the faithful what happens in a man's soul when he is ordained a priest. John Vianney displays the priest's capacity to change the world by transforming a small corner of it through preaching and the sacraments.

I wonder what John Vianney would have said if he had been told that 150 years after his death, priests and seminarians from the four corners of the earth would travel to Ars to pray to him for holiness and zeal. He likely would have dismissed the thought and turned his mind back to Jesus and his parishioners.

Considering the life of the Curé of Ars, priests and laity alike realize the amazing things God can do to build up the Church through his ministers. John Vianney allowed himself to be totally transformed by the character of holy orders. In reality, we know little about him except that he was a priest of Jesus Christ and is the "peerless model" for all priests.

4

The Priest:
A Man Configured to Jesus Christ

Scores of people came to Ars on pilgrimage during the forty-one years of the pastorate of Saint John Vianney to meet a priest of Jesus Christ. Some came, no doubt, because there was hype in the air about the Curé of Ars. "He reads hearts", they said. "He tells you your sins before you even begin your confession. He understands all human problems. When you confess to him, you feel the presence and the love of God. There are many healings, spiritual and physical, all around him. Look at all those crutches on the walls of the church!"

Just as some people flocked to Christ to see a show, so they came to Ars. Most people, it seems, traveled to Ars because they believed—or at least wanted to believe—in Jesus Christ. During the last decade or so of John Vianney's life, approximately a thousand people came to the parish church of Ars every week to confess their sins. By faithfully hearing confessions every day, the Curé of Ars became and remains the icon of priestly zeal for confession. Although he was sometimes direct and challenging in confession, John Vianney is most remembered for his gentleness and compassion as a confessor. The Catholic people intuited that

Christ sat in the confessional of Ars raising those who were spiritually dead in sin to life in the Holy Spirit.

Although he is best known for these gifts, John Vianney had many other endowments of grace. People came to Ars to hear his strong and affective preaching, among them the famous preacher Lacordaire. Pope John XXIII, in his encyclical letter *From the Beginning of Our Priesthood* (no. 81), describes Vianney's preaching:

> Up to the time of his blessed death, Saint John Vianney held on tenaciously to his office of teaching the faithful committed to his care and the pious pilgrims who crowded the church, by denouncing evil of every kind, in whatever guise it might appear, "in season, out of season" and, even more, by sublimely raising souls to God; for "he preferred to show the beauties of virtue rather than the ugliness of vice." For this humble priest understood perfectly how great the dignity and sublimity of teaching the word of God really is. "Our Lord"—he said—"who Himself is truth, has as much regard for His word as for His Body."

Pilgrims who visit the parish church of Ars notice not only a pulpit but also a catechetical desk. In accordance with the directives of the Council of Trent, the saint was convinced that everyone, not only children preparing for first penance, first Communion, and confirmation, needs to be fortified in the fundamental truths of the faith through catechetical instruction. And so the pastor of Ars gave catechetical lessons every Sunday and, in fact, nearly every day of the week.

His guideposts were the Apostles' Creed, the Church's summary of all God has done in salvation history; catechesis on the seven sacraments; a careful explanation of how

to live according to the Ten Commandments; and instruction on prayer by means of a thorough explanation of the
Our Father, petition by petition. Surely the favorite topic
of the Curé of Ars was the Holy Eucharist.

Interestingly, Vianney preached and catechized using the
content and methodology that the Fathers of the Church
had used as they presided over the catechumenate, the same
content and method proposed by the *Catechism of the Council of Trent* as well as the current *Catechism of the Catholic
Church* and the *General Directory for Catechesis*. Vianney knew
that his fidelity to Catholic doctrine ensured that his preaching would be both apostolic and charismatic. This fidelity
to the apostolic faith would guarantee the presence and activity of Christ and the Holy Spirit in his preaching and
catechesis.

As pastor, John Vianney proved that apostolic success in
a parish is very much bound up with the faithful transmission of Catholic doctrine through preaching and catechetical instruction. The saint passed on the faith in the way
that the Church has always transmitted her belief from the
time of the apostles. When a parish priest neglects or relin-
quishes his responsibility for the catechesis of his people,
both he and his parishioners are sadly impoverished.

In his latter years, Father Vianney often preached about
the love of Jesus in the Eucharist both from the pulpit and
from the catechist's desk. For him, the sacrament of penance was the way back to Holy Communion for those who
had fallen into grave sin. Confession was also the road to
more-fruitful reception of the Holy Eucharist for those living in the grace of God. The saint understood that the
Christian's capacity to love God and neighbor is increased
by every worthy reception of Holy Communion. It was as
clear as day to John Vianney: Just as the Lamb of God is the

light and center of the heavenly Jerusalem, so the Eucharist is the living, vibrant center of the Church. Everything the priest does, he does for Christ in the Eucharist.

People made the pilgrimage to Ars to participate in the priest's Mass. Seeing him celebrate the Mass, one would have no doubt: He was offering sacrifice to God, the one sacrifice of Christ for the redemption of the world. In his Letter to Priests for Holy Thursday of 1986, Pope John Paul II described the place of the Mass in the spiritual life of the Curé of Ars:

> The Eucharist was at the very center of Saint John Vianney's spiritual life and pastoral work. He said: "All good works put together are not equivalent to the Sacrifice of the Mass, because they are the works of men and the Holy Mass is the work of God." It is in the Mass that the sacrifice of Calvary is made present for the Redemption of the world. Clearly, the priest must unite the daily gift of himself to the offering of the Mass: "How well a priest does, therefore, to offer himself to God in sacrifice every morning!" "Holy Communion and the Holy Sacrifice of the Mass are the two most efficacious actions for obtaining the conversion of hearts."

> Thus the Mass was for John Mary Vianney the great joy and comfort of his priestly life. He took great care, despite the crowds of penitents, to spend more than a quarter of an hour in silent preparation. He celebrated with recollection, clearly expressing his adoration at the consecration and communion. He accurately remarked: "The cause of priestly laxity is not paying attention to the Mass!" (8)

In the same letter, the Holy Father describes the place of adoration of the Blessed Sacrament in the life of the saint:

The Curé of Ars was particularly mindful of the permanence of Christ's real presence in the Eucharist. It was generally before the tabernacle that he spent long hours in adoration, before daybreak or in the evening; it was towards the tabernacle that he often turned during his homilies, saying with emotion: "He is there!" It was also for this reason that he, so poor in his presbytery, did not hesitate to spend large sums on embellishing his church. The appreciable result was that his parishioners quickly took up the habit of coming to pray before the Blessed Sacrament, discovering, through the attitude of their pastor, the grandeur of the mystery of faith. (8)

John Vianney was regularly engaged in the works of charity. He faithfully visited the sick and the dying. He gave all he had to the poor who either lived in his parish or passed through it. He started a school for the education of poor children. The apple of his eye was the "Providence", an orphanage he founded for girls.

The Curé of Ars drew others, both religious and laity into his works of charity. He was the father of the poor and the needy, living in poverty himself for their sake. One sees in him Christ reaching out and loving those who have no one else to care for them. For him, it was inconceivable for a priest to offer the Eucharist and not devote himself to the works of charity demanded by the needs of his parishioners.

The Fathers of the Second Vatican Council deepened the Church's understanding of the character of holy orders. Before the Council, it was customary for theologians and spiritual writers to describe the character as the priestly powers of consecration of the Eucharist and absolution of sins in the sacrament of penance. Through the teaching found in the Decree on the Life and Ministry of Priests (*Presbyterorum Ordinis*) and subsequent magisterial statements, it is now common to assert that through the character of holy orders, the priest is the living instrument of Jesus Christ, not only in the administration of the sacraments—though that is his primary role—but also in preaching and teaching the Catholic faith and offering pastoral care to his people.

Saint John Vianney is a wonderful exemplar of this teaching. People recognized that Christ preached when the Curé of Ars preached, that Christ catechized when the Curé catechized, that Christ nurtured the sick and the poor through the priest's pastoral care of his flock, and that Christ applied the merits of his passion and death through the celebration of the sacraments.

In ordination, the priest receives both the character and the grace of the priesthood. The character of holy orders distinguishes the ordained from the nonordained members of the Christian faithful (*signum distinctivum*) and establishes them in a permanent leadership role in the Church. The one character of holy orders is also the foundation of the distinctions and relationships that exist among the three ranks of the sacrament of holy orders: the episcopacy, the presbyterate, and the diaconate.

The character of holy orders configures the priest to Christ and empowers him to make Christ present whenever he preaches the gospel, administers the sacraments, and brings the love of Jesus, the Good Shepherd, to his people in the various forms of pastoral charity. The character of holy orders is a spiritual, interior, and ontological sign that configures the priest to Christ in his headship over the Church (*signum configurativum*). Even if the priest carries out his priestly duties in the state of unrepentant mortal sin, he is nonetheless able to act in the Person of Christ precisely through the character that configures him permanently to Christ.

There have been many efforts to explain the special sacramental grace proper to holy orders. In the past, theologians explained that the grace of the priesthood includes
an increase of sanctifying grace, a strengthening of the theological and moral virtues and gifts of the Holy Spirit for
ministry, and a pledge of all the actual graces necessary for
faithfully living out the priestly vocation over the course
of a lifetime. Without denying the validity of this explanation, some have sought to explain the sacramental grace
of orders as a participation in Christ's pastoral charity for
his flock.

While the character of holy orders is, in essence, the capacity the priest receives in ordination to render the Paschal
Mystery of Christ effective and fruitful in people's lives, the
sacramental grace of holy orders is the infusion of pastoral
charity. In other words, in ordination, the priest not only
becomes a living instrument of Jesus Christ but also receives
a share of the Good Shepherd's love for his flock. The priest
manifests this love of Christ and grows in personal holiness
precisely by preaching the Word of God, administering the
sacraments, and giving pastoral care to God's people.

The grace of holy orders flows from the character and
serves it. In giving the priest the capacity to make Christ
present in his Paschal Mystery, God likewise gives him a
supernatural impulse, the desire, to do what priests are
ordained to do. This offers insight into the traditional teaching that the character is a sign that disposes (*signum dispositivum*). The character is also a sign that obligates the priest
(*signum obligativum*) to exercise his priesthood as the Good
Shepherd of the flock. As a result of his new relationship
with Christ, the priest is obliged to pursue the perfection
of charity through the free observance of the gospel counsels of poverty, chastity, and obedience.

The bishop articulates this truth in the ordination homily: "Your ministry will perfect the spiritual sacrifice of the faithful by uniting it to Christ's sacrifice, the sacrifice that is offered sacramentally through your hands. Know what you are doing and imitate the mystery you celebrate. In the memorial of the Lord's death and resurrection, make every effort to die to sin and to walk in the new life of Christ."[1]

When a man gives himself to Christ in ordination, Our Lord pledges to give him all the graces he needs to grow in pastoral charity every day of his life. He also receives the grace to live faithfully in the celibate state. It is important for the priest to understand the omnipresent help of God in living out his vocation, especially since similar graces are given to Christian spouses in the sacrament of matrimony and to men and women consecrated to God through the profession of the evangelical counsels. The priest as spiritual father of his flock gives assurance to all that God's grace is sovereign and always available.

The personality of the Curé of Ars was fully permeated and transformed by the grace of holy orders. He not only made present Christ's sacrifice in Mass and confession but re-presented his Lord in everything he did. His intense life of prayer, penance, and radical availability to the people, especially in the confessional, manifested the grace of Jesus, the Good Shepherd, and made his priestly ministry abundantly fruitful.[2]

---

[1] As mentioned earlier, the bishop emphasizes this truth when he hands the newly ordained priest the paten holding unleavened bread and the chalice filled with wine and water: "Accept from the holy people of God the gifts to be offered to him. Know what you are doing, imitate the mystery you celebrate: model your life on the mystery of the Lord's cross."

[2] Pope John Paul II, in his 1986 Letter to Priests for Holy Thursday, explained how the priest's personal holiness helps his people to grow in their

Those who made the pilgrimage to Ars instinctively recognized that Jesus was living and working there. They found his love in the Curé's heart.

---

relationship with Christ: "John Mary Vianney sanctified himself so as to be more able to sanctify others. Of course, conversion remains the secret of hearts, which are free in their actions, and the secret of God's grace. By his ministry, the priest can only enlighten people, guide them in the internal forum and give them the sacraments. The sacraments are of course actions of Christ, and their effectiveness is not diminished by the imperfection or unworthiness of the minister. But the results depend also on the dispositions of those who receive them, and these are greatly assisted by the personal holiness of the priest, by his perceptible witness, as also by the mysterious exchange of merits in the Communion of Saints. Saint Paul said: 'In my flesh I complete what is lacking in Christ's afflictions for the sake of his body, that is, the Church' (Col 1:24). John Mary Vianney in a sense wished to force God to grant these graces of conversion, not only by his prayer but by the sacrifice of his whole life. He wished to love God for those who did not love him, and even to do the penance which they would not do. He was truly a pastor completely at one with his sinful people" (11).

5

Saint John Vianney:
A Rich Man without a Penny

Jesus Christ calls every member of his Church, without exception, to the perfection of Christian charity, that is, evangelical holiness. The articulation of this truth, with its roots deep in the gospel, was and remains perhaps the most revolutionary statement of the Fathers of the Second Vatican Council. They taught in the Dogmatic Constitution on the Church (*Lumen Gentium*), chapter 5, that in baptism all are called to Christian perfection, and they also explained the role of the evangelical counsels in the life of all Christians.[1] Although relatively few in the Church are called to profess publicly the gospel counsels of poverty, chastity, and obedience, all must embrace them to some degree to attain the perfection of charity.

By practicing the evangelical counsels, the Christian removes obstacles to the full development of the love of God and neighbor. Simplicity of life, chastity according to one's state of life, and obedience to Christ through his Church facilitate the growth of supernatural charity. Consecrated men and women (religious) embrace the counsels

---

[1] See also Saint Thomas Aquinas, *Summa Theologiae* II-II, q. 184, a. 3, and *Catechism of the Catholic Church*, nos. 1972–74.

43

publicly and live in community to exemplify gospel values for all the members of the Church. The layperson freely embraces the counsels in various degrees to bear witness credibly to Christ and his gospel in the secular world. The diocesan priest, unlike the religious priest, does not profess public vows of poverty, chastity, and obedience. However, at his ordination, he publicly promises lifelong celibacy and obedience to his bishop. The experience of the saints convinces the diocesan priest that detachment from material possessions and a simple lifestyle facilitate pastoral charity.

Priests respond to Saint Paul's admonition by their observance of the evangelical counsels: "I appeal to you therefore, brethren, by the mercies of God, to present your bodies as a living sacrifice, holy and acceptable to God, which is your spiritual worship. Do not be conformed to this world but be transformed by the renewal of your mind, that you may prove what is the will of God, what is good and acceptable and perfect" (Rom 12:1–2).

The Decree on the Life and Ministry of Priests (*Presbyterorum Ordinis*) of Vatican II extols the value of gospel poverty in the life of all priests. One might imagine that the Fathers of the Council had John Vianney in mind as they described this counsel in the life of a diocesan priest:

> Priests are invited to embrace voluntary poverty. By it they become more clearly conformed to Christ and more ready to devote themselves to their sacred ministry. The apostles by their example gave testimony that the free gift of God was to be given freely. Guided then by the Holy Spirit of the Lord, who anointed the Savior and sent him to preach the Gospel to the poor, priests and bishops alike are to avoid everything that might in any way antagonize the poor. More than the rest of Christ's disciples they are to put aside all appearance of vanity in their surroundings. They are to

arrange their house in such a way that it never appears unapproachable to anyone and that nobody, even the humblest, is ever afraid to visit it. (17)

Although Saint John Vianney grew in his observance of the evangelical counsels over the course of his forty-one years as pastor of Ars, poverty, chastity, and obedience were set in place in his life well before the day of his priestly ordination. His spiritual director, Father Charles Balley, had wonderfully modeled them for him as he exercised the diocesan priesthood in the rectory of Ecully. There are amusing stories of competition between the two over points of ascetical practice. As a result of Father Balley's example and the movements of the Holy Spirit in his own soul, John Vianney came to his priestly ordination well trained in the observance of the counsels. Vianney's membership in the Third Order of Saint Francis later in his life illustrates his admiration for the simplicity and radical poverty of the "poor man of Assisi" whose lifestyle he emulated as a diocesan priest.

For Vianney, the counsel of poverty is the imitation of Christ, who chose to own nothing and depend on the Providence of his Father for all his needs: "A scribe came up and said to him, 'Teacher, I will follow you wherever you go.' And Jesus said to him, 'Foxes have holes, and birds of the air have nests; but the Son of man has nowhere to lay his head'" (Mt 8:19–20).

He heard the challenge to embrace gospel poverty in Christ's words to the rich young man as recorded by Saint Matthew:

One came up to him, saying, "Teacher, what good deed must I do, to have eternal life?" And he said to him, "Why do you ask me about what is good? One there is who is good. If you would enter life, keep the commandments." He said to him, "Which?" And Jesus said, "You shall not kill, You shall not commit adultery, You shall not steal, You shall not bear false witness, Honor your father and mother, and, You shall love your neighbor as yourself." The young man said to him, "All these I have observed; what do I still lack?" Jesus said to him, "If you would be perfect, go, sell what you possess and give to the poor, and you will have treasure in heaven; and come, follow me." When the young man heard this he went away sorrowful; for he had great possessions. (Mt 19:16–22)

John Vianney grew up in a poor farming family where simplicity of life was his daily fare. This prepared him to embrace a simple lifestyle as a priest. Taking Christ's words literally, "If you would be perfect, go, sell what you possess and give to the poor, and come, follow me", he gave whatever money, food, or material possessions that were given to him to the poor. He used the entire inheritance he received from his father to build his "Providence", a home and school for orphaned girls. He was convinced that whatever was given to him belonged to Christ and to the Church and, in a special way, to the poor. Early in his priestly life, he acquired the virtue of giving everything away. Like Christ, the Curé of Ars wanted to die owning nothing.

Pope Benedict XVI, in his letter written to all priests on the occasion of the beginning of the Year for Priests[2] (June 2009–June 2010), offers a moving description of the poverty of the Curé of Ars and describes the evangelical poverty that is appropriate for the diocesan priest:

The Curé of Ars lived the "evangelical counsels" in a way suited to his priestly state. His *poverty* was not the

---

[2] Letter Proclaiming a Year for Priests on the 150th Anniversary of the "Dies Natalis" of the Curé of Ars, June 16, 2009. The complete text of this letter may be found in Appendix 1 of this book.

poverty of a religious or a monk, but that proper to a priest: while managing much money (since well-to-do pilgrims naturally took an interest in his charitable works), he realized that everything had been donated to his church, his poor, his orphans, the girls of his "*Providence*", his families of modest means. Consequently, he "was rich in giving to others and very poor for himself". As he would explain: "My secret is simple: give everything away; hold nothing back". When he lacked money, he would say amiably to the poor who knocked at his door: "Today I'm poor just like you, I'm one of you". At the end of his life, he could say with absolute tranquillity: "I no longer have anything. The good Lord can call me whenever he wants!'

There are three temptations that priests and future priests need to recognize and fight against in their lives. Each is a temptation to put some object in the place that only Christ should have in the life of his priest. It is safe to say that each of these temptations builds upon the other, creating a monstrous idol that, in the end, looks surprisingly like its maker! John Vianney's way of life offers a strong antidote for these illnesses of the soul.

The first temptation is a fixation on "stuff". Because the diocesan priest in the United States, wherever he may live, has more than enough money, it is easy for him to live as a gentleman of the upper middle class, a comfortable bachelor. Let us ponder the sad and empty song of clerical materialism. The foundation of the melody is clerical entitlement. It goes something like this: "For all my sacrifices, I deserve a fine car, the best restaurants, expensive vacations, a house in the country or at the shore, all the latest electronic devices, a stout portfolio of stocks and bonds, a television in nearly every room, a well-stocked liquor cabinet, a pet or pets, a steady round of golf at fancy country clubs, and, needless to say, a rectory more lavish in its appointments than most other residences in the parish." The tragedy is that some priests do not realize how scandalized the people are by clerical worldliness and how incompatible it is with the image of the priesthood as lived by Jesus Christ and his servant John Vianney.

Second, there is the clerical temptation to put honors at the center of everything. It appears that there may be some priests, perhaps many, who would rather be recognized publicly and loudly applauded for their achievements by the bishop, civic leaders, organizations, and parishioners rather than accumulate stuff. More likely, stuff and the quest for honors live in the same house.

A particularly lethal form of this temptation is lust for the episcopacy, a vice that surely never entered the mind of the Curé of Ars, who was sufficiently overwhelmed by the grace and responsibilities of the priesthood. Sad to say, some bishops have contributed to the fund of clerical worldliness by their example. One wonders if one North American seminary or another over the years has not promoted a political approach to the priesthood and ambition for the episcopacy among the clergy.

Abbé François Trochu, in his biography *The Curé d'Ars*, humorously describes John Vianney's reactions to the honors he received late in his life. In 1852 the bishop of Belley, Monsignor Chalandon, conferred the title of honorary canon of the cathedral chapter of Belley on the Curé of Ars. In our world, this would mean that the bishop named him a monsignor. The bishop came to Ars with the vicar general to invest John Vianney with the cape (mozzetta) associated with his new title. As soon as the bishop left town, Vianney took off the cape, never to wear it again, and began negotiations to sell it in order to obtain money for the poor of his parish. Always a transparent priest, Vianney wrote a letter explaining his action to the bishop: "Monseigneur, the mozetta which you have had the great charity to bestow on me has given me much pleasure, because, being in want of money to complete a foundation, I have sold it for fifty francs. That price completely satisfied me." [3] Trochu noted, "Notwithstanding the most pressing solicitations, M. Vianney would at no time consent to appear in the dress of a canon, not even in the presence of his Bishop." [4]

In 1855 the emperor Napoleon named John Vianney a member of the Royal Order of the Legion of Honor for his many works of charity in Ars and its environs by awarding him the Golden Cross of that order. When the mayor broke the news, the Curé, without displaying either satisfaction or surprise, asked, "Is there a pension attached to that cross? Does it mean money for my poor?" The mayor answered, "No; it is just a distinction", to which the saint responded, "Very well, since the poor have nothing to gain by it, tell the Emperor, please, that I do not want it." [5]

Later, when told that he was expected to send twelve francs to pay for the certificate of knighthood and postage for the cross, Vianney said, "No, never! ... Have I not refused it? I prefer to spend that money to-day in feeding twelve poor persons!" [6] A parishioner by the name of Toccanier paid the twelve francs without telling the saint. When the cross arrived, he said, "I did not send the money and yet *they* have sent me the cross all the same." [7] Trochu observes

---

[3] Abbé Francis Trochu, *The Curé d'Ars: Saint Jean-Marie-Baptiste Vianney*, trans. Dom Ernest Graf, O.S.B. (Rockford, Ill.: TAN Books, 1977), pp. 390–91.

[4] Ibid., p. 391.

[5] Ibid., p. 393.

[6] Ibid., p. 394.

[7] Ibid.

that the poor Curé of Ars "refused to have the cross pinned
to his cassock, so that the only time he ever wore it was
when it was placed on his coffin." [8] The Curé explained
why he was so resolute in rejecting ecclesiastical and civil
honors: "What if when death comes and I present myself
with these baubles, God were to say to me: 'Begone, you
have had your reward on earth'?" [9]

Finally, there is the temptation to create a personality cult.
All priests are leaders of God's people. We may say that
many priests and seminarians are "alpha males", men wired
to lead. This is, in a sense, the way it should be. However,
it is possible for a pastor to enjoy his leadership position
much more than he should.

There are danger signs that indicate that a priest may be
promoting himself and not his Lord. Does he draw most of
his energy from the adulation of the people rather than from
preaching the gospel and leading people to Christ in the
sacraments? Does he obsessively demand the undivided attention and love of his parishioners? Does he feel jealous and
threatened when he is not the center of attention? When
he has a microphone in his hands, is he his favorite topic?

An elderly priest once compared these huge clerical per-
sonalities to those hot-air balloons that come floating down
Fifth Avenue in Manhattan as part of the annual Thanksgiving Day parade. The personal tastes of the pastor or parochial vicar, his eccentricities, hobbies, consuming interests,
style of humor, even his pet, are easily enlarged and forced
on the entire parish. When this happens, the people's focus
is easily turned away from Christ and toward the enor-
mous, and likely needy, ego of the pastor. Some will be

[8] Ibid., p. 395.
[9] Ibid., p. 393.

drawn to the "hot-air balloon" personality, at least for a while. Many will be disenchanted rather quickly.

There is a significant breach of priestly poverty whenever any or all of this happens. When the magnification of the pastor's personality diminishes the visibility of Christ in him, there is the inversion of authentic priestly mediation: The priest uses Christ in some way to draw people to himself and to the "riches" of his own personality. The opposite is the goal: Everything about the priest should attract people to Christ and invite them to union with the Lord. The priest's personality is important but merely as a bridge that leads people to Christ.

It is difficult, is it not, to formulate a concept of the personality of the Curé of Ars? Everything we know about him bespeaks mediation of Christ. His selfless, transparent mediation led his parishioners to love him, and to love him intensely. However, he did not allow it to stop there. Everything he said and did drew the people of Ars to Jesus.

The priest, if he is to have a fruitful, supernatural ministry, must learn how to love his people in such a way that in loving him in return, they experience union with Christ. This is the art of being a mediator of the one Mediator. The parish priest seeks to be transparent, drawing people not to himself but rather, through himself, to Jesus. To deliberately draw people to oneself and to stop there is perhaps the most serious violation of priestly poverty possible.

Why was John Vianney able to avoid the pitfalls of materialism in the three forms we just discussed: accumulation of material goods; quest for honors, both ecclesiastical and civil; and the establishment of a personality cult? John Vianney recognized that there is no greater possession, no greater honor, no personality more fascinating than the Divine Person of the Word. In possessing Christ as a priest and knowing how to mediate Christ's riches to his people, Vianney felt that he was the richest man on earth.

Compared to the wonder of his spiritual fatherhood, through which he gave his people the divine life of grace and nurtured that life, worldly pleasures such as material possessions, human honors, and the promotion of his own personality meant nothing to him. In fact, the more generously Father Vianney gave everything away for the sake of his people, the more he was able to generate spiritual children through his priesthood. He realized that real poverty engenders a beautiful, freeing dependence on Providence, inviting the Father in heaven to manifest his generosity and paternal tenderness toward his children. Filling one's life with "stuff" as a priest, feverishly seeking honors, and promoting the cult of self may indicate a lack of trust in the Providence of God and, at a deeper level, a defect in the virtue of faith. The crucial question is: *Why isn't Christ enough?*

Along with Paul the apostle, John Vianney considered everything as garbage, as rubbish compared to knowing and possessing Christ and sharing in his priesthood:

> Whatever gain I had, I counted as loss for the sake of Christ. Indeed I count everything as loss because of the surpassing worth of knowing Christ Jesus my Lord. For his sake I have suffered the loss of all things, and count them as refuse, in order that I may gain Christ and be found in him, not having a righteousness of my own, based on law, but that which is through faith in Christ, the righteousness from God that depends on faith; that I may know him and the power of his resurrection, and may share his sufferings, becoming like him in his death, that if possible I may attain the resurrection from the dead. (Phil 3:7–11)

6

Saint John Vianney:
A Celibate Man with Scores of Children

Saint Matthew records a discussion Jesus had with the Phari-
sees and his disciples on the indissolubility of marriage and
on the mystery of virginity or celibacy for the sake of the
Kingdom of heaven. This scriptural text is the foundation
of the Church's understanding of the evangelical counsel of
chastity:

> Pharisees came up to him and tested him by asking, "Is
> it lawful to divorce one's wife for any cause?" He
> answered, "Have you not read that he who made them
> from the beginning made them male and female, and
> said, 'For this reason a man shall leave his father and
> mother and be joined to his wife, and the two shall
> become one'? So they are no longer two but one. What
> therefore God has joined together, let no man put asun-
> der." They said to him, "Why then did Moses com-
> mand one to give a certificate of divorce, and to put her
> away?" He said to them, "For your hardness of heart
> Moses allowed you to divorce your wives, but from the
> beginning it was not so. And I say to you: whoever
> divorces his wife, except for unchastity, and marries
> another, commits adultery; and he who marries a divorced
> woman, commits adultery."

The disciples said to him, "If such is the case of a man with his wife, it is not expedient to marry." But he said to them, "Not all men can receive this precept, but only those to whom it is given. For there are eunuchs who have been so from birth, and there are eunuchs who have been made eunuchs by men, and there are eunuchs who have made themselves eunuchs for the sake of the kingdom of heaven. He who is able to receive this, let him receive it." (Mt 19:3–12)

In becoming man, the Son of God chose celibacy as his own way of life. He asked the twelve apostles, even though they were married, to leave everything to follow him. Paul, likewise, was celibate and extolled the celibate way of life for those to whom it is given by the Holy Spirit.

Clearly, for Christ and Paul, and the other apostles, celibacy is a special grace from God, a gift that is and will continue to be given to men called to share in Christ's mission. The gift of celibacy is given for the sake of building up the Kingdom of God on earth. The celibate makes present and visible in the world the life that all of the redeemed will experience in heaven after the resurrection of the dead on the Last Day.

Throughout the ages, the Church in both the East and West has conferred episcopal ordination only on priests who have received the gift of celibacy. In the West, the Church confers presbyteral ordination only on men who have received the gift of celibacy. Pope Benedict XVI has noted that this requirement is a sign of the transcendent origin of the apostolic ministry in the Church from the beginning. The priesthood is not something the Church provides for herself. It is a gift that comes from God.

Needless to say, the charism of celibacy is not restricted only to those men who share in the apostolic ministry. God offers the gift to many men and women who devote themselves exclusively to Christ and his concerns. John Vianney had many collaborators in his priestly work: male and female religious as well as single men and women who were free to devote themselves wholeheartedly to the pastor's works of charity.

Before we examine the gift of celibacy properly so called, we need to consider what the Church presumes of celibate priests and men preparing for the priesthood.

First of all, celibacy is the free renunciation of marriage and natural parenthood for the service of Christ and the Church. Celibacy presumes the chastity that is common to all the baptized members of the Church who participate in the Holy Eucharist. Adultery, fornication, homosexual acts, masturbation, viewing pornography, and engaging in any deliberate impure thoughts and desires are all incompatible with the grace of baptism and are therefore incompatible with the Christian life.

Second, celibacy presumes a high level of affective maturity. The celibate priest and seminarian, for instance, need to understand the difference between ministering to a woman he finds sexually attractive and ministering to a woman *because* he finds her sexually attractive. The healthy celibate recognizes his motivation in every situation. The celibate priest will serve women he finds sexually appealing. However, when a priest focuses his time and energy on a woman he finds attractive and excludes the unattractive from his ministry, he is in danger of using the body of Christ for his own sexual gratification—at least in his mind.

The celibate needs to recognize when a pastoral friendship with a woman or pastoral collaboration in an apostolate is a conscious or unconscious cover-up for what, in reality, is a dating relationship. He needs to acknowledge when he is flirting with a woman and when a woman is flirting with him. The priest who does not carefully guard his heart and who does not know how to establish proper boundaries in a celibate lifestyle is doomed to "crash and burn" early in his priesthood, leaving a trail of devastation behind.

Suffice it to say that the grace of celibacy presupposes and is built on the foundation of genital chastity and affective maturity, but it includes much more than these foundational prerequisites.

To have a clear view of the grace of celibacy, we need to look at it from a number of different perspectives. I will suggest three. First, a man rightly chooses celibacy for the sake of a personal and intimate relationship with Christ. Saint Paul acknowledged this motivation in the First Letter to the Corinthians: "I want you to be free from anxieties. The unmarried man is anxious about the affairs of the Lord, how to please the Lord; but the married man is anxious about worldly affairs, how to please his wife" (1 Cor 7:32–33). This means that the celibate should be wholeheartedly devoted to prayer and indefatigable in his endeavors to build up the Church, Christ's body, in every way possible.

Saint John Vianney's life of celibacy was built on the firm foundation of fidelity to prayer and a relentless drive to build the Church of Christ, especially through the ministry of the Word and sacraments. In his priestly ministry, Vianney understood that the energy to practice celibacy has a supernatural source: deep prayer and zeal for the salvation of souls.

Interestingly, Pope Benedict, in his Letter Proclaiming a Year for Priests (June 16, 2009), notes that the Eucharist is the foundation of the priest's chastity: "Saint John Vianney's chastity, too, was that chastity demanded of a priest for his ministry. It could be said that it was a chastity suited to one who must daily touch the Eucharist, who contemplates it blissfully and with that same bliss offers it to his flock. It was said of him that 'he radiated chastity'; the faithful would see this when he turned and gazed at the tabernacle with loving eyes."

Second, celibacy is a means of sharing in Christ's life-giving passion and death for the salvation of his Church. Celibacy, lived well, is never easy. We can be certain that it was not easy for the Curé of Ars. It will not be easy for any priest precisely because celibacy is a participation in the passion of Christ for the salvation of souls.

Saint Paul spoke of the mystery of the suffering of the minister of Christ that is a channel of supernatural life for the beneficiaries of the ministry. Surely, Paul spoke in a global way of the hardships involved in preaching the gospel. However, it is not farfetched to imagine that he included celibacy as a part of the whole picture. Paul died to self every day through his celibacy so that the people to whom he preached could have abundant life in Christ:

> For it is the God who said, "Let light shine out of darkness," who has shone in our hearts to give the light of the knowledge of the glory of God in the face of Christ.
>
> But we have this treasure in earthen vessels, to show that the transcendent power belongs to God and not to us. We are afflicted in every way, but not crushed; perplexed, but not driven to despair; persecuted, but not forsaken; struck down, but not destroyed; always carrying in the body the death of Jesus, so that the life of Jesus may also be manifested in our bodies. For while we live we are always being given up to death for Jesus' sake, so that the life of Jesus may be manifested in our mortal flesh. So death is at work in us, but life in you.

Since we have the same spirit of faith as he had who
wrote, "I believe, and so I spoke," we too believe, and
so we speak, knowing that he who raised the Lord Jesus
will raise us also with Jesus and bring us with you into
his presence. For it is all for your sake, so that as grace
extends to more and more people it may increase thanksgiving, to the glory of God.

So we do not lose heart. Though our outer man is
wasting away, our inner man is being renewed every day.
For this slight momentary affliction is preparing for us
an eternal weight of glory beyond all comparison, because
we look not to the things that are seen but to the things
that are unseen; for the things that are seen are transient,
but the things that are unseen are eternal. (2 Cor 4:6–18)

I recently heard a group of young married men speaking
about how they deal with sexual temptations in their lives.
Although I did not question them, I am certain they were
referring to temptations such as impure thoughts, inappro-
priate glances, perhaps looking at pornography, or flirting
with their co-workers. They explained that whenever they
are tempted in any way, they seek, through grace, to reject
the temptation, and they offer the mortification involved in
overcoming their desires as an act of love for their wives
and as a prayer for the chastity of their sons and daughters.
What a wonderful application of Saint Paul's spiritual principle: I die to myself, so that others may have life in Christ!

Priests and future priests would be well advised to embrace
this practice. Whenever a celibate is tempted to violate his
promise of celibacy in any way, he should consciously reject
the temptation, offering the victory over self to God for
those parishioners who are struggling with chastity. This is
what Saint Paul means, I believe, when he says, "Death is
at work in us, but life in you."

Pope Paul VI, in his encyclical on priestly celibacy, wrote that married couples merit chastity for their priests through their practice of marital chastity. Conversely, priests merit marital chastity for their people through their fidelity to celibacy. The priest's celibacy is for the sanctification of his people.

Third, celibacy is a powerful source of spiritual fatherhood. Many spiritual realities contributed to Saint John Vianney's remarkable ability to generate children in the order of grace: his fidelity to prayer; his penances, which seem so extreme to us today; his generosity and availability to the people; and his faith in the sacraments. However, near the top of the list in importance is his fidelity to celibacy for the love of Christ and the Church. From the practical point of view, if John Vianney had had a wife and children, he never would have been able to devote so much time to the confessional. Over and above this simple fact, we might say that it was his celibacy that drew men and women to him like a magnet, perhaps especially men and women struggling with sexual sins.

In a mysterious way, celibacy contributes to the priest's capacity to be the instrument in the healing of the wounds of human nature and in the generation of divine life in souls. By freely renouncing natural fatherhood, the priest takes up the mission of generating supernatural life in souls through the preaching of the Word and the administration of the sacraments. Many are convinced that the Catholic people confess their sins so freely to their priests precisely because of the grace of celibacy. If this is true, then one may only imagine how pure was the heart of John Vianney, who drew so many people through his fatherly heart to the heart of Christ. His spiritual fatherhood not only restored supernatural life to souls in the sacrament of penance but

also, through that restoration of divine life, ensured the penitents' physical resurrection from the dead on the day of
Christ's return in glory. In this sense, the priest's spiritual
fatherhood will have an amazing physical effect on the Last
Day.

On the day of his funeral, unbelievers surely thought of
John Vianney as a lonely old man without progeny, yet more
than a thousand of his children attended his funeral and
wept for the man who had given them the gift of eternal
life in baptism or who had restored it, when lost through
mortal sin, in the sacrament of penance. How many men
and women will rise from the grave on the Last Day and
enter the Kingdom of heaven in the flesh because of the
ministry of Saint John Vianney? When they meet him, they
will call him Father.

7

Saint John Vianney: Model of the Obedience of Christ

In the Letter to the Philippians, Saint Paul calls attention to the obedience of Christ and holds him up as the exemplar of humility and obedience for all Christians:

> Though he was in the form of God, did not count equality with God a thing to be grasped, but emptied himself, taking the form of a servant, being born in the likeness of men. And being found in human form he humbled himself and became obedient unto death, even death on a cross. Therefore God has highly exalted him and bestowed on him the name which is above every name, that at the name of Jesus every knee should bow, in heaven and on earth and under the earth, and every tongue confess that Jesus Christ is Lord, to the glory of God the Father. (Phil 2:6–11)

The Church prays this canticle at Evening Prayer on the vigil of each Sunday of the year. It summarizes Christ's Paschal Mystery in few words: The Son of God emptied himself of glory, becoming man, and humbled himself even more, being obedient, even to death on a cross. As a consequence, the Father exalted Christ in his Resurrection, revealing him as Lord of all creation.

In the sacrament of baptism, the Christian is incorporated into Christ, becoming a son or daughter of the Father in the Lord Jesus. At the same time, the Christian is incorporated into Christ's saving death and Resurrection and is given the capacity to obey the Father and surrender to him through the grace of Christ. It is worth noting again that the hymn just cited connects humility and obedience in Jesus: "He humbled himself and became obedient unto death."

In his account of the Last Supper, the beloved disciple records an event not mentioned by the other Evangelists. At the beginning of the meal, Jesus, performing the task of a slave, washed the feet of his apostles:

> Now before the feast of the Passover, when Jesus knew that his hour had come to depart out of this world to the Father, having loved his own who were in the world, he loved them to the end. And during supper, when the devil had already put it into the heart of Judas Iscariot, Simon's son, to betray him, Jesus, knowing that the Father had given all things into his hands, and that he had come from God and was going to God, rose from supper, laid aside his garments, and tied a towel around himself. Then he poured water into a basin, and began to wash the disciples' feet, and to wipe them with the towel that was tied around him. He came to Simon Peter; and Peter said to him, "Lord, do you wash my feet?" Jesus answered him, "What I am doing you do not know now, but afterward you will understand." Peter said to him, "You shall never wash my feet." Jesus answered him, "If I do not wash you, you have no part in me." Simon Peter said to him, "Lord, not my feet only but also my hands and my head!" Jesus said to him, "He who has bathed does not need to wash, except for his feet, but he is clean all over; and you are clean, but not all of you." For he knew who was to betray him; that was why he said, "You are not all clean."

When he had washed their feet, and taken his garments, and resumed his place, he said to them, "Do you know what I have done to you? You call me Teacher and Lord; and you are right, for so I am. If I then, your Lord and Teacher, have washed your feet, you also ought to wash one another's feet. For I have given you an example, that you also should do as I have done to you. Truly, truly, I say to you, a servant is not greater than his master; nor is he who is sent greater than he who sent him. If you know these things, blessed are you if you do them."
(Jn 13:1–17)

Here we have a kind of icon of the Lord's humility and obedience that symbolizes and explains the meaning of the passion narrative that follows: Christ designates himself as the priest and victim of the sacrifice of the new covenant and consecrates the Twelve to share in his mission as priest and victim in the High Priestly Prayer (Jn 17). He institutes the Eucharist and the priesthood in one integral act of creation. The glorification of the Son of Man begins at the supper through the betrayal of Judas. The washing of the apostles' feet, a gesture startling and dramatic, reveals Jesus as the Suffering Servant of the Lord who "in his hour" restores man to divine sonship through the shedding of his blood.

Stated simply, Jesus did what his Father asked him to do for the salvation of the human race. As the innocent Lamb of God, he accepted everything involved in the passion and obeyed his Father perfectly. The author of the Letter to the Hebrews states that all who will be saved are saved precisely by the obedience of Christ:

In the days of his flesh, Jesus offered up prayers and supplications, with loud cries and tears, to him who was able to save him from death, and he was heard for his

godly fear. Although he was a Son, he learned obedience through what he suffered; and being made perfect
he became the source of eternal salvation to all who obey
him, being designated by God a high priest according to
the order of Melchizedek. (Heb 5:7–10)

And in another place, the author of Hebrews explains that
Christians are saved by the obedience of Christ:

For since the law has but a shadow of the good things to
come instead of the true form of these realities, it can never,
by the same sacrifices which are continually offered year
after year, make perfect those who draw near. Otherwise,
would they not have ceased to be offered? If the worship-
ers had once been cleansed, they would no longer have any
consciousness of sin. But in these sacrifices there is a
reminder of sin year after year. For it is impossible that the
blood of bulls and goats should take away sins.
   Consequently, when Christ came into the world, he said,
      "Sacrifices and offerings you have not desired,
      but a body have you prepared for me;
      in burnt offerings and sin offerings you have taken
         no pleasure.
      Then I said, 'Behold, I have come to do your will,
         O God,'
      as it is written of me in the roll of the book."
When he said above, "You have neither desired nor taken
pleasure in sacrifices and offerings and burnt offerings and
sin offerings" (these are offered according to the law), then
he added, "Behold, I have come to do your will." He abol-
ishes the first in order to establish the second. And by that
will we have been sanctified through the offering of the
body of Jesus Christ once for all. (Heb 10:1–10)

"By that will we have been sanctified"! The author of the
Letter to the Hebrews tells us that we are saved by Christ's

obedience and that we are able to respond in obedience and love to the Father only by entering into, only by sharing in, the will of Christ crucified. Clearly, the Christian is sanctified by this will of Christ and shares in it through baptism. The man ordained a priest lives the virtue and the counsel of obedience through pastoral charity.

We shall contemplate three levels of obedience in the priest's life through the lens of Saint John Vianney's life. Each degree of obedience is built upon the previous degree and transforms the priest, making him more like Christ in both his obedience and humility.

As there are presuppositions regarding priestly chastity, so there are presuppositions that go ahead of the practice of the evangelical counsel of obedience and support it. A priest or seminarian cannot understand and live the counsel of obedience until these rudiments of the Christian life have been firmly set in place. They include a firm commitment to obey the Commandments of God in imitation of Christ and through the power of his grace, the practice of restoring or strengthening his share in Christ's obedience through the frequent reception of the sacrament of penance, the desire to fulfill the duties of his state of life (pastoral work for the priest, study and everything involved in formation for the seminarian), acceptance of the crosses that God sends or permits in his life, respect for and attentiveness to the teaching office of the successor of Saint Peter and the successors of the apostles, and, included in this, readiness to adhere to the Church's canon and liturgical law.

John Vianney believed that in obeying his diocesan bishop, he would discover and accomplish the will of God. When the bishop assigned him to Ars, the poorest and most remote parish in the diocese, Vianney believed that God was sending him there. The bishop told him, through the vicar general: "There is not much love for God in that parish; you will bring some into it." [1] He received these words as coming from the mouth of Christ himself. Consequently, as pastor of Ars, he developed a plan: earnest daily prayer with strong doses of penance offered for the conversion of his parishioners. Being a practical man, he set two immediate goals: First, he would visit all his parishioners with his eye on increasing their attendance at Sunday Mass. Second, he would preach and catechize to eliminate the religious illiteracy that existed in the aftermath of the French Revolution.

Everything that happened in Ars over the next forty-one years was the result of John Vianney's obedience to his bishop. He had listened closely to the voice of Christ speaking through the bishop: "There is not much love for God in that parish; you will bring some into it." Note well that the word *obedience* in its root means "to listen", "to be attentive". The priest must be convinced that Christ will assign him a specific mission through his bishop. On occasion, this listening will necessitate a frank discussion between bishop and priest and, on the part of the priest, the willingness to express himself honestly to the bishop and then *obey*.

John Vianney did not naïvely believe that bishops are infallible in their pastoral judgments and decisions. He acknowledged that bishops can and do make mistakes in guiding their priests.

In 1848 his bishop decided that the Curé of Ars would be relieved of the administration of the "Providence", the orphanage and school the saint had founded in the parish. It was decided that the Sisters of Saint Joseph would take over the administration of the orphanage and the school.

---

[1] Abbé Francis Trochu, *The Curé of Ars: Saint Jean-Marie-Baptiste Vianney*, trans. Dom Ernest Graf, O.S.B. (Rockford, Ill.: TAN Books, 1977), p. 101.

This decision of the bishop distressed John Vianney and the three women who had long been his collaborators at the Providence. The Providence had been Vianney's oasis of peace during the years when throngs of people came each week to confess to the saint. Vianney had his lunch every day with the orphans, visited the children on the playground, and taught them catechism. He also gave regular direction to the three women who managed the day-to-day operations of the Providence. Father Vianney looked forward to his retirement in the orphanage.

There had been intimations that the Curé and these dedicated Catholic women were no longer capable of giving proper care to the girls in their charge. The bishop wanted to help the Curé of Ars by placing the orphanage and the school in the hands of religious who had been professionally prepared for the task of the Christian education of youth. As the negotiations proceeded, it became obvious that the sisters, perhaps in agreement with the bishop himself, intended to hold the orphanage in abeyance until it could be reestablished on a better footing later. The sisters' main focus would be the administration and staffing of the school. The Curé's vision of an orphanage and a school for the poor girls of his parish vanished before his eyes. In the midst of the trial, he admitted: "The Bishop ... sees the will of God in all this, but I fail to see it." [2] Trochu notes, "At length he agreed to all that was asked of him, and he did so gladly and wholeheartedly." [3]

This episode in Saint John Vianney's life demonstrates a solid principle of priestly obedience: Bishops can and do

---

[2] Ibid., p. 367.
[3] Ibid.

make mistakes in their pastoral judgments. It would be naïve and unhealthy for a priest to believe that bishops do not err in administrative or pastoral matters. John Vianney did not agree with the bishop's decision to take the administration of the Providence out of his hands. He expressed his concern to the bishop with the understanding that he would obey the bishop's decision as the will of God for him.

While acknowledging that the bishop can be mistaken in his judgments, Vianney recognized that the priest never makes a mistake in obeying his bishop. Dying to self by the renunciation of his will, the priest obeys the bishop for the love of God. This renunciation causes him to grow in personal holiness. His obedience became a powerful source of pastoral fruitfulness in his ministry.

Blessed John XXIII, in the encyclical *From the Beginning of Our Priesthood*, described the supernatural motive of Vianney's obedience:

> It should be noted that this full obedience of John Vianney to the commands of his superiors rested on supernatural principles; in acknowledging and duly obeying ecclesiastical authority, he was paying the homage of faith to the words of Christ the Lord as He told His Apostles "He who hears you, hears me." To conform himself faithfully to the will of his superiors he habitually restrained his own will, whether in accepting the holy burdens of hearing Confessions, or in performing zealously for his colleagues in the apostolate such work as would produce richer and more saving fruits. (29)

The Curé of Ars knew that as a priest, he was a co-worker of the bishops, who succeed the apostles. He understood that he could not be an obedient steward of the mysteries of God without seeking to transmit the tradition that comes to us from the apostles. For this reason, he knew he needed to study Catholic doctrine and moral teaching frequently so that he would be capable of passing the Catholic faith on in its fullness and purity to his people. Although John Vianney had serious trouble with his studies in the seminary, he did not abandon personal study after ordination.

Saint John Vianney understood that the promise of obedience he had made on the occasion of his ordination was a pledge to obey the local bishop and his successors. He appreciated, though, that the promise symbolized something greater. The priest's mission is to re-present and transmit the faith that has been held by the college of bishops from Pentecost until the present moment as a faithful co-worker of that college. The promise of obedience is a commitment to hand on the Catholic faith in its fullness to the Christian people. This includes teaching them the proper interpretation of the Old and New Testaments through evangelization, catechesis, liturgical preaching, and theology; the celebration of the Eucharistic Sacrifice and sacraments of the Church as the tradition understands and celebrates them; and the cultivation of the Christian way of life in its totality as established by the apostles. Our saint understood that the promise of obedience meant all of this.

The diocesan priest observes the evangelical counsel of obedience when he does what the bishop asks him to do even though he might want to do something else. Three times during his forty-one years in his parish, John Vianney, feeling the personal need to retire to live a more contemplative lifestyle, ran away from Ars. Even though he had been extraordinarily faithful to his life of prayer as a parish priest, he felt the need for more prayer and penance. The first flight took place after approximately twenty-five years in Ars; the second and third, after approximately thirty-five and thirty-six years in the parish. In each instance, Vianney intended either to join a monastic order or live in solitude away from parochial duties.

People have speculated on the possible causes of these mysterious flights from Ars:

- The Curé of Ars felt acutely the pressure of his pastoral responsibility, experienced a kind of "spiritual panic attack", and ran away.
- He felt overwhelmed by the numbers of people who crowded around him day in and day out without a moment of reprieve. He sensed that he was drowning in an ocean of pastoral work and never had any breathing space for himself.
- Since his youth, Vianney had a desire for quiet, solitude, uninterrupted prayer, and penance, and so he felt the need to weep for his poor life and prepare for death.
- He had difficulty understanding that his hours in the confessional were a kind of continuous communion with Christ in the mystery of the redemption, a very high form of contemplative love of God and neighbor.
- He experienced some form of psychological or emotional fragility. It is perfectly understandable that a man who had heard confessions for over twelve hours a day would be frazzled by the intensity of the work at hand. Interestingly, when he returned to Ars after the most embarrassing attempt at desertion, he admitted: "I behaved like a child." [4]

[4] Bartholomew O'Brien, *The Curé of Ars*. (Rockford, Ill.: TAN Books, 2007), p. 90.

- Likely, exacerbating all of the components listed here, the devil sought to undo the good work of the Curé of Ars. He did this, as always, by lying, using lines such as: "You are endangering your own salvation with all of these confessions. You need to get away. Take care of yourself. Solitude is God's will for you. By obeying the bishop, you are disobeying God."

Each time that John Vianney ran away from Ars to seek solitude, he turned back, realizing that the Lord, through his bishop, had asked him to bring the love of God to the people of Ars. At these points in his life, Father Vianney's will and God's will crossed, and Vianney allowed God to win. The only light of discernment he had was the stated will of the bishop.

Pope Benedict XVI, in his Letter Proclaiming a Year for Priests (June 16, 2009), describes the temptations of the Curé of Ars—and his victory through priestly obedience:

Saint John Mary Vianney's *obedience* found full embodiment in his conscientious fidelity to the daily demands of his ministry. We know how he was tormented by the thought of his inadequacy for parish ministry and by a desire to flee "in order to bewail his poor life, in solitude". Only obedience and a thirst for souls convinced him to remain at his post. As he explained to himself and his flock: "There are no two good ways of serving God. There is only one: serve him as he desires to be served". He considered this the golden rule for a life of obedience: "Do only what can be offered to the good Lord".[5]

---

[5] Blessed John XXIII, in his encyclical *Sacerdotii Nostri Primordia*, also explained the luminous obedience of the Curé of Ars: "All his life he longed to lead a quiet and retired life in the background, and he regarded pastoral duties as a very heavy burden laid on his shoulders and more than once he tried to free himself of it. His obedience to his bishop was admirable; We would like

Did the recently ordained John Vianney, when he began his work in Ars with a group of approximately 230 rough and religiously illiterate parishioners, think of Christ bending down and washing the feet of his disciples? Did he ever turn to this mystery when, fatigued by hours in the confessional, he studied dogmatic and moral theology to transmit the faith more effectively to his people? When the exhausted Vianney walked away from Ars under the cover of night to find solace in solitude and prayer, did he again gaze upon the obedient Christ washing his disciples' feet and hear him say: "Truly, truly, I say to you, a servant is not greater than his master; nor is he who is sent greater than he who sent him. If you know these things, blessed are you if you do them" (Jn 13:16–17)?

Vatican II's Decree on the Life and Ministry of Priests (*Presbyterorum Ordinis*) describes the obedience of Saint John Vianney in a very powerful way: "Among the virtues especially demanded by the ministry of priests must be reckoned that disposition of mind by which they are always prepared to seek not their own will but the will of him who has sent them" (15).

---

to mention a few instances of it in this encyclical, Venerable Brethren: 'From the age of fifteen on, he ardently desired a solitary life, and as long as this wish was not fulfilled, he felt cut off from every advantage and every consolation that his state of life might have offered': but 'God never allowed this aim to be achieved. Undoubtedly, this was God's way of bending Saint John Mary Vianney's will to obedience and of teaching him to put the duties of his office before his own desires; and so there was never a time when his devotion to self-denial did not shine forth'; 'out of complete obedience to his superiors, John M. Vianney carried out his tasks as pastor of Ars, and remained in that office till the end of his mortal life'" (28).

8

The Sacrament of Reconciliation as a Re-presentation of the Passion of Christ

During the last decade of Saint John Vianney's life, tens of thousands of penitents came to him every year for absolution. It was normal for him to spend twelve, fifteen, or more hours a day in the confessional. This striking phenomenon prompts a question: What precisely was the grace of the Curé of Ars? Various answers have been proposed. Some believe that John Vianney was chosen to be the sign of God's mercy in the years following the terror of the French Revolution. Might it have been his mission to absolve the sins committed during those dark, diabolical years in France? Considered in a broader context, perhaps Christ chose John Vianney to bless the Church with a renewed awareness of the role of the sacrament of penance in the Christian's sanctification. Through the example of Vianney, a bright light was cast on the indispensable ministry of the parish priest. So many of the faithful, ordained and laity, venerate the Curé of Ars because he reminds them that the shepherd becomes holy by caring for his flock. The charism of John Vianney seems to be a striking coalescence of all these graces, as well as others hidden in the mind of God.

Early in his priesthood, Vianney began to experience the opposition of Satan—or the *Grappin*, as he called him.

Although the parish priest often did battle in his room at night with Satan, he understood that the real battle with the evil one and the victory over him took place whenever he raised his hands over his penitents and said the words, "I absolve you from your sins." The priest came to understand that violent diabolical attacks often signaled the approach of a penitent who desperately needed forgiveness. The more noise the devil made, the more convinced the saint was that a man or woman carrying a heavy burden of sin was approaching Ars. He sometimes joked that the devil and he were collaborators.

Saint John Vianney heard confessions so devotedly because he believed and experienced that the sacrifice of Calvary is somehow made truly present in the sacrament of penance. Although he may not have expressed it this way, the Curé of Ars lived his life as a priest at the heart of the Paschal Mystery of Christ both by celebrating the Holy Eucharist and by hearing confessions. Some might find this assertion novel and perhaps startling. "Yes," the well-catechized Catholic might respond, "the Mass re-presents, that is, makes present, the mystery of the Lord's suffering, death, and Resurrection in a sacramental manner, but does confession really do the same?"

It is safe to say, I believe, that few are aware of the fact that there is indeed the re-presentation of the Cross and Resurrection of Christ in the sacrament of penance. This re-presentation of the Lord's Passover does not take place as it does at Mass under the signs of bread and wine offered to God and consecrated by the priest but rather takes place deep within the penitent through a remarkable and often painful engagement of mind, heart, and emotion in Christ's suffering.

It is helpful to look at the *Catechism of the Catholic Church* for the precise explanation of the term *re-presentation* ("making present") as it is used in sacramental theology:

In the liturgy of the Church, it is principally his own Paschal mystery that Christ signifies and makes present. During his earthly life, Jesus announced his Paschal mystery by his teaching and anticipated it by his actions. When his hour comes, he lives out the unique event of history that does not pass away: Jesus dies, is buried, rises from the dead, and is seated at the right hand of the Father "once for all." His Paschal Mystery is a real event that occurred in our history, but it is unique: all other historical events happen once, and then they pass away, swallowed up in the past. The Paschal mystery of Christ, by contrast, cannot remain only in the past, because by his death he destroyed death, and all that Christ is—all that he did and suffered for all men—participates in the divine eternity, and so transcends all times while being made present in them all. The event of the Cross and Resurrection *abides* and draws everything toward life.[1]

The *Catechism of the Catholic Church* is asserting that the Paschal Mystery of Christ is made present in the liturgical celebration of every sacrament. The grace of his saving death and Resurrection is applied in different ways to the recipient of the sacrament, enriching him spiritually. The presence of Christ and his grace also enrich the minister of the sacrament with an increase of charity.

The Fathers of the Church spoke of the sacrament of penance as a "laborious baptism". They at least implicitly affirmed that penance brings an exceptional share in Jesus' expiatory death. The theologian Leo Scheffczyk wrote, "In the sacramental drama of penance, what takes place is nothing less than that the sinner joins the suffering Christ; he enters into the mind and the work of the expiating Savior, even if the difference remains, which must never be

---

[1] *Catechism of the Catholic Church*, 1085.

overlooked, that the sinner, unlike Christ, does this for his personal sins which are thoroughly his own." [2]

Through the acts of the penitent, namely, contrition, humble confession, and willingness to make satisfaction for the sins committed, the Holy Spirit causes a personal and intimate configuration to Christ in his passion. In fact, it is precisely this re-presentation of the Paschal Mystery in the depths of the human heart that restores the penitent who has committed grave sin to friendship with God and reopens the way to integral participation in the Eucharistic sacrifice. The sacrament of penance also empowers the penitent who confesses venial sins to offer the sacrifice of the Mass more fruitfully and with greater love.

John Vianney, who was engaged so intensely in hearing confessions, instinctively recognized the mysterious presence of the crucified Christ in the sacrament of penance. An episode that occurred late in his life, an event that we will consider later, suggests that John Vianney's spiritual path was a mysticism rooted in his mediation of the redemption in confession. The saint likewise grasped the profound connection between confession and the Holy Eucharist. He understood that his ministry of reconciliation helped the faithful participate worthily and fruitfully in the sacramental re-presentation of Christ's sacrifice at Mass. Vianney's life illustrates that every authentic work of the priest, especially hearing confessions, is oriented to the Holy Sacrifice of the Mass.

Pope Benedict XVI, in his 2009 Letter Proclaiming a Year for Priests, notes the intimate connection between the Eucharistic Sacrifice and sacramental confession in the life of the

---

[2] Leo Scheffczyk, *The Specific Saving Effect Proper to the Sacrament of Penance* (Rome: International Community "The Work of Christ", 1996), pp. 15–16.

priest. Perhaps Pope Benedict XVI decided to name Saint John Vianney the patron saint of *all* priests and not just of parish priests to make the point forcefully that all priests are ordained chiefly to re-present the sacrifice of the Cross in the Holy Eucharist and in the sacrament of reconciliation:

Saint John Vianney's deep personal identification with the Sacrifice of the Cross led him—by a sole inward movement—from the altar to the confessional. Priests ought never to be resigned to empty confessionals or the apparent indifference of the faithful to this sacrament. In France, at the time of the Curé of Ars, confession was no more easy or frequent than in our own day, since the upheaval caused by the revolution had long inhibited the practice of religion. Yet he sought in every way, by his preaching and his powers of persuasion, to help his parishioners to rediscover the meaning and beauty of the sacrament of Penance, presenting it as an inherent demand of the Eucharistic presence. He thus created a *"virtuous" circle*. By spending long hours in church before the tabernacle, he inspired the faithful to imitate him by coming to visit Jesus with the knowledge that their parish priest would be there, ready to listen and offer forgiveness. Later, the growing numbers of penitents from all over France would keep him in the confessional for up to sixteen hours a day. It was said that Ars had become "a great hospital of souls". His first biographer relates that "the grace he obtained [for the conversion of sinners] was so powerful that it would pursue them, not leaving them a moment of peace!" The saintly Curé reflected something of the same idea when he said: "It is not the sinner who returns to God to beg his forgiveness, but God himself who runs after the sinner and makes him return to him". "This good Saviour is so filled with love that he seeks us everywhere".

Reflection on the passion of Christ helps the priest and, indeed, every Christian understand the unique re-presentation of Christ's sacrifice in the sacrament of reconciliation. Christ's suffering on the Cross was, above all, an act of worship of the Father on behalf of sinful men. His dying is the sacrifice that merits redemption, makes satisfaction for sin, and brings salvation.[3] Through the application of the merits of Christ's suffering and death, the Holy Spirit offers every human person the grace of justification, sanctification, and the gift of eternal life. It is this act of worship that becomes present in the Holy Eucharist in an eminent way. We want to shed light on how the crucified Christ's worship of the Father becomes present and effective in the sacrament of penance.

In meditating on the passion of Christ, the Christian instinctively first considers the physical pain of Jesus. John Henry Newman's description of Christ's agony opens the door to the consideration of the three levels or degrees of suffering that Christ endured in his passion: the physical torture of crucifixion, the mental agony of bearing the guilt of every human sin as his own, and the suffering of love:

> His head was crowned and torn with thorns, and bruised with staves; His face was defiled with spitting; His shoulders were weighed down with the heavy cross; His back was rent and gashed with scourges; His hands and feet gored through with nails; His side . . . wounded with the spear; His mouth parched with intolerable thirst. . . . And thus He hung upon the cross for six hours, His whole body one wound, exposed almost naked to the eyes of

[3] Saint Thomas Aquinas, *Summa Theologiae* III, q. 48, a. 1–4.

men, "despising the shame," and railed at, taunted, and cursed by all who saw Him.[4]

In spite of the immensity of the physical agony that Christ endured in the scourging, the crowning with thorns, the nailing of his hands and feet to the Cross, and the long hours of torture as he hung stretched out between heaven and earth, these bodily sufferings were, in fact, the least of what he endured to expiate sins not his own.

The prophet Isaiah foretold that the "Suffering Servant" of the Lord, the Messiah, would bear the guilt of the sins of the world. On Good Friday, the Church contemplates the prophet's teaching: "The LORD has laid on him the iniquity of us all" (Is 53:6). The Servant of the Lord, in accepting his Father's will, took upon himself the guilt of human sin. Christ not only carried every sin to the Cross but also assumed the guilt of sin through an act of astounding substitution. Citing the fourth Suffering Servant song of Deutero-Isaiah in his First Letter, Saint Peter writes, "He himself bore our sins in his body on the tree, that we might die to sin and live to righteousness. By his wounds you have been healed" (1 Pet 2:24).

Although it is not in vogue in some areas of the Church in the United States and elsewhere to hold that Christ saw and assumed the guilt for all sin in his passion, the weight of the theological tradition of the Church affirms that the crucified Savior, seeing his Father face-to-face in his human consciousness, therein intimately encountered every person in need of salvation.[5]

---

[4] John Henry Newman, B.D., *Parochial and Plain Sermons*. (San Francisco: Ignatius Press, 1997), p. 1218.

[5] The *Catechism of the Catholic Church*, 151, affirms: "Because he 'has seen the Father,' Jesus Christ is the only one who knows him and can reveal

Describing this mystery, Cardinal J. Francis Stafford, in an address to the Society for Catholic Liturgy on September 21, 2006, said:

> According to the usage of Saint Augustine, the Latin word *confessio* refers not only to *confessio peccati* (confession of sin), but also to *confessio laudis* (confession of praise) and to *confessio fidei* (confession of faith). Jesus habitually confessed, admits, and reveals himself through these three confessions before the Father to be his only begotten Son. Always and everywhere he confesses himself to be the gift of the Father. For the Father is his source and origin. The acme of Jesus' confessional drama was reached during his passion and death. Then the Sinless One voluntarily underwent an "exchange of places" with all the sinners of the world. In the Last Supper, Jesus prayed, "Father, the hour has come: glorify your Son that the Son may glorify You" (Jn 17:1). Aware of his unique relation to the Father, he accepted the unimaginable burden of the whole world's "no" to God. Every human being throughout history has loaded his or her sins upon the Innocent One whose outstretched arms embraced them all in love.[6]

The crucified Christ did not see sin in a general or collective way. He saw sinners one by one and felt the guilt of every sin as if it were his own.[7] Born of his experience of Christ as his Savior, Saint Paul preached: "I have been

---

him." Paragraph 473 of the *Catechism* likewise speaks of the "intimate and immediate knowledge that the Son of God made man has of his Father".

[6] Cardinal J. Francis Stafford, "Sacraments of Healing: Reconciliation and Anointing", *Antiphon: A Journal for Liturgical Renewal* 11, no. 1 (2007): 9.

[7] *Catechism of the Catholic Church*, 478: "Jesus knew and loved us each and all during his life, his agony, and his Passion and gave himself up for each one of us: 'The Son of God ... loved me and gave himself for me. He has loved us all with a human heart.' For this reason, the Sacred Heart of Jesus, pierced by our sins and for our salvation, 'is quite rightly considered the

crucified with Christ; it is no longer I who live, but Christ who lives in me; and the life I now live in the flesh I live by faith in the Son of God, who loved *me* and gave himself for *me*" (Gal 2:20; emphasis added).

Saint Paul described the depths of Christ's mental agony in the passion with penetrating insight: "For our sake [God] made him to be sin who knew no sin, so that in him we might become the righteousness of God" (2 Cor 5:21). The sinless Son of God in his *kenosis* was so identified with sin that the apostle boldly affirmed that Christ *became sin* to cleanse sinners and make them holy.[8]

By exploring Saint Paul's assertion that Christ took every sin as his own so that all people might be transformed in his holiness, the Christian begins to understand the intimate link between the passion of Christ and sacramental confession. Penance is the place of exchange where he who suffered for sin gives the person of faith a share in his holiness.

In a sermon entitled "The Mental Sufferings of Our Lord in His Passion", John Henry Newman expresses the Church's understanding of Christ's suffering. He graphically attempts to describe how Our Lord experienced every act of revolt

---

chief sign and symbol of that ... love with which the divine Redeemer continually loves the eternal Father and all human beings' without exception."

[8] Hans Urs von Balthasar described this level of suffering in one of his sermons on the passion: "Jesus, the Crucified, endures our inner darkness and estrangement from God, and he does so in our place.... There is nothing familiar about it to him: it is utterly alien and full of horror. Indeed, he suffers more deeply than an ordinary man is capable of suffering, even were he condemned and rejected by God, because only the incarnate Son knows who the Father really is and what it means to be deprived of him and to have lost him (to all appearances) forever" (Hans Urs von Balthasar, *You Crown the Year with Your Goodness: Radio Sermons*, trans. Graham Harrison [San Francisco: Ignatius Press, 1989], p. 85).

against God as his own in the passion. The text, phenom-
enological in temper, displays sparks of literary genius. More
important, it invites an exploration of how the God-man
embraced every person in the passion:

There, then, in that most awful hour, knelt the Savior of
the world, putting off the defenses of His Divinity, dis-
missing His reluctant Angels, who in myriads were ready
at His call, and opening His arms, baring His breast, sinless as He was, to the assault of His foe,—of a foe whose
breath was a pestilence, and whose embrace was an agony.
There He knelt, motionless and still, while the vile and
horrible fiend clad His spirit in a robe steeped in all that
is hateful and heinous in human crime, which clung close
around His heart, and filled His conscience, and found
its way into every sense and pore of His mind, and spread
over Him a moral leprosy, till He almost felt Himself to
be that which he never could be, and which His foe
would fain have made Him. Oh, the horror, when He
looked, and did not know Himself, and felt as a foul and
loathsome sinner, from His vivid perception of that mass
of corruption which poured over His head and ran down
even to the skirts of His garments! Oh, the distraction,
when He found His eyes, and hands, and feet, and lips,
and heart, as if the members of the Evil One, and not
of God! Are these the hands of the immaculate Lamb
of God, once innocent, but now red with ten thousand
barbarous deeds of blood? Are these His lips, not uttering prayer, and praise, and holy blessings, but as if
defiled with oaths, and blasphemies, and doctrines of dev-
ils? Or His eyes, profaned as they are by all the evil visions
and idolatrous fascinations for which men have abandoned their Adorable Creator? And His ears, they ring
with sounds of revelry and of strife; and His heart is
frozen with avarice, and cruelty, and unbelief; and His

very memory is laden with every sin which has been committed since the fall, in all regions of the earth, with the pride of the old giants, and the lusts of the five cities, and the obduracy of Egypt, and the ambition of Babel, and the ingratitude and scorn of Israel. Oh, who does not know the misery of a haunting thought that comes again and again, in spite of rejection, to annoy, if it cannot seduce? Or of some odious and sickening imagination, in no sense one's own, but forced upon the mind from without? Or of evil knowledge, gained with or without a man's fault, but which he would give a great price to be rid of at once and for ever? And adversaries such as these gather around Thee, Blessed Lord, in millions now; they come in troops more numerous than the locust or the palmer-worm, or the plagues of hail, and flies, and frogs, which were sent against Pharaoh. Of the living and of the dead, of the as yet unborn, of the lost and of the saved, of Thy people and of strangers, of sinners and of saints, all sins are there.

It is the long history of a world, and God alone can bear the load of it. Hopes blighted, vows broken, lights quenched, warnings scorned, opportunities lost: the innocent betrayed, the young hardened, the penitent relapsing, the just overcome, the aged failing; the sophistry of misbelief, the willfulness of passion, the obduracy of pride, the tyranny of habit, the canker of remorse, the wasting fever of care, the anguish of shame, the pining of disappointment, the sickness of despair; such cruel, such pitiable spectacles, such heart-rending, revolting, detestable, maddening scenes; nay, the haggard faces, the convulsed lips, the flushed cheek, the dark brow of the willing victims of rebellion, they are all before Him now; they are upon Him and in Him. They are with Him instead of that ineffable peace which has inhabited His soul from the moment of His conception. They are upon Him, they are all but His own; He cries to His Father as if He were the criminal, not the victim; His agony takes the form of guilt and compunction. He is doing penance. He is making confession, He is exercising contrition with a reality and a virtue infinitely greater than that of all the saints and penitents together; for He is the One Victim for us all, the sole Satisfaction, the real Penitent, all but the real sinner.[9]

Christ endured the physical suffering of the Cross and bore the whole burden of human sin motivated by a love beyond description, a love at once human and divine. The crucified Christ was on fire with love for his Father, whom he glorified in the passion. In his sufferings, Christ saw and loved each member of the human race, thirsting for a relationship with all for whom he shed his blood.

Blessed Teresa of Calcutta, carried by the current of the Church's interpretation of Scripture, heard in Christ's cry from the Cross, "I thirst", the longing of his human heart for the love of all the men he redeemed. In the encyclical *Lord and Giver of Life*, Pope John Paul II explains that the Holy Spirit descended into Christ's sacrifice, igniting such a fire of love in the redeemer's heart that he became a "holocaust of love".[10]

[9] John Henry Cardinal Newman, *Sermons and Discourses* (1839–1857; repr., New York: Longmans, Green, 1949), pp. 242–45. Note the teaching in paragraph 603 of the *Catechism of the Catholic Church*: "Jesus did not experience reprobation as if he himself had sinned. But in the redeeming love that always united him to the Father, he assumed us in the state of our waywardness of sin, to the point that he could say in our name from the cross: 'My God, my God, why have you forsaken me?' Having thus established him in solidarity with us sinners, God 'did not spare his own Son but gave him up for us all,' so that we might be 'reconciled to God by the death of his Son.' "

[10] "The Old Testament on several occasions speaks of 'fire from heaven' which burnt the oblations presented by men. By analogy one can say that the Holy Spirit is the 'fire from heaven' which works in the depth of the mystery of the Cross. Proceeding from the Father, he directs toward the

It was his love that gave infinite value to his physical and mental suffering.

Acknowledging that Christ experienced an intimate communion with every human person in his passion, it becomes clear that his suffering in its totality is *satisfaction* for sins. Taking each transgression of God's law as if it were his own, the innocent Lamb of God's sorrow for sin took the form of *contrition*. His intimate appropriation of the sin of every person took the form of *confession*. As Newman preached: "His agony takes the form of guilt and compunction. He is doing penance. He is making confession, He is exercising

---

Father the sacrifice of the Son, bringing it into the divine reality of the Trinitarian communion. If sin caused suffering, now the pain of God in Christ crucified acquires through the Holy Spirit its full human expression. Thus there is a paradoxical mystery of love: in Christ there suffers a God who has been rejected by his own creature: 'They do not believe in me!'; but at the same time, from the depth of this suffering—and indirectly from the depth of the very sin 'of not having believed'—the Spirit draws a new measure of the gift made to man and to creation from the beginning. In the depth of the mystery of the Cross, love is at work, that love which brings man back again to share in the life that is in God himself.

"The Holy Spirit as Love and Gift comes down, in a certain sense, into the very heart of the sacrifice that is offered on the Cross. Referring here to the biblical tradition, we can say: He consumes this sacrifice with the fire of the love that unites the Son with the Father in the Trinitarian communion. And since the sacrifice of the Cross is an act proper to Christ, also in this sacrifice he 'receives' the Holy Spirit. He receives the Holy Spirit in such a way that afterwards—and he alone with God the Father—can 'give him' to the Apostles, to the Church, to humanity. He alone 'sends' the Spirit from the Father. He alone presents himself before the Apostles in the Upper Room, 'breathes upon them' and says: 'Receive the Holy Spirit; if you forgive the sins of any, they are forgiven,' as John the Baptist had foretold: 'He will baptize you with the Holy Spirit and with fire.' With those words of Jesus, the Holy Spirit is revealed and at the same time made present as the Love that works in the depths of the Paschal Mystery, as the source of the salvific power of the Cross of Christ, and as the gift of new and eternal life" (John Paul II, *Lord and Giver of Life*, 41).

contrition with a reality and a virtue infinitely greater than that of all the saints and penitents together; for He is the One Victim for us all, the sole Satisfaction, the real Penitent, all but the real sinner."

With a proper understanding of the doctrine of substitution, what conclusion might be drawn from Saint Paul's teaching that Christ "became sin" so that the sinner might become "the righteousness of God"? The answer is found only in the Catholic teaching on the efficacy of sacramental absolution. The penitent's contrition for sin, his confession to the Church's minister, and the willingness to do penance are nothing less than a share in the contrition, confession, and satisfaction of the crucified Lord. The absolution of the priest completes and perfects the acts of the penitent by joining imperfect acts of contrition, confession, and satisfaction to Christ's perfect work of charity on Calvary. Through this real communion with the sufferings of Christ, the penitent passes through the Cross to experience forgiveness in the mystery of the Resurrection.[11]

Saint John Vianney understood that the primary agent in the celebration of the sacrament of penance is the Holy Trinity—the Father working through his Son by the power of the Holy Spirit. Through the grace of the Paschal Mystery, Our Lord touches and moves the penitent long before he steps into the confessional. Actual grace is so abundant and diverse that it is difficult to explain the different ways that people are drawn to Christ in sacramental confession. At times, the grace comes through the preaching of the Word of God that is "living and active, sharper than any two-edged sword, piercing to the division of soul and spirit, of joints and marrow, and discerning the thoughts and intentions of the heart"

---

[11] See Pope John Paul II, *Redemptor Hominis*, 20.

(Heb 4:12). Possibly grace manifests itself as a piercing aware-ness of the possibility of eternal loss in hell, the painful expe-rience of a relationship destroyed or damaged by transparent self-centeredness, the recognition of a disturbing duplicity, a sudden consciousness of the ugliness of sin and the harm it inflicts on oneself and others, or an inner perception of the goodness of God along with the desire to be at peace with him in the present and in eternity. It is a great grace for the sinner to experience interiorly that the pleasure of union with God is far better than the gratification afforded by any sin.

These and similar experiences indicate that God's grace is being given to and received by a sinner, inspiring repen-tance (Rom 5:5). Whether the sorrow the Christian feels is based on an egocentric concern for salvation (imperfect con-trition) or on the love of God (perfect contrition), these feelings are indications that the Holy Spirit is drawing the person back to union with the Father through Christ. Con-trition, imperfect or perfect, is always the manifestation of the grace of Christ in the heart of a sinner.

Although these and similar experiences of grace indicate that the Holy Spirit is ultimately attracting a person to Christ in the Eucharist, that individual, because of sin, often must first pass through the gate of the sacrament of reconcilia-tion. When a penitent approached him, Father Vianney was acutely aware that the grace of God had long been at work in him bringing him to the moment of sacramental encoun-ter with the Lord. The saint was likewise conscious that Christ in his Paschal Mystery was the magnet drawing the sinner to himself, first in the confessional and then in the Eucharist. As representing Christ and the Church, the Curé of Ars understood that his mission was to complete the work of grace by re-presenting the sacrifice of the Cross, first for the forgiveness of sins in confession, and then in the

Eucharistic sacrifice. The same Christ is at work in both sacraments, each ordered to the other!

How does the Christian enter into the saving passion of Christ through sacramental confession? The penitent first makes an act of faith by confessing his sins to a priest. The penitent comes, acknowledging that the priest represents both Christ and the Church. Explicit in every confession is the recognition on the part of the penitent that sin both offends God and wounds the Church.[12]

Many, if not most, of the people who came to Ars for confession bore heavy burdens of sin or at least had serious problems in their lives. Why else would they have traveled so far and waited so long to spend a few moments alone with Father Vianney? Journeying to Ars, the penitents instinctively acknowledged what the Fathers of the Council of Trent had taught definitively: According to divine law, the baptized Christian who has committed mortal sins must present them honestly in confession by kind and number.[13]

---

[12] The risen Christ, by breathing upon the apostles and saying to them, "Receive the Holy Spirit. If you forgive the sins of any, they are forgiven; if you retain the sins of any, they are retained" (Jn 20:22–23), drew them into his love for the Father and for the sinful human race. In giving the apostles his power to forgive sins, Christ made them collaborators in his work of restoring supernatural life to mankind. Christ instituted the sacrament of penance in order that reconciliation with God would be mediated in and through his Church's ministers. It was this capacity to forgive sins, transmitted by the bishop, the successor of the apostles, through the laying on of hands that propelled John Vianney to offer his life as a holocaust of love in the confessional.

Obviously, the sinfulness and worldliness of priests scandalizes the faithful and destroys their confidence in the sacrament of penance. Many of the contemporaries of John Vianney who had been unable or reluctant to find Christ in the pre-Revolution Church that had become so closely aligned with the noble classes of French society readily found him in the poor, chaste, and obedient parish priest of Ars and rushed to confess their sins to him.

[13] *Code of Canon Law*, 940: "Individual and integral confession and absolution constitute the only ordinary way by which the faithful person who is

Scores of people came to Ars because they were eager to confess their sins to the Curé, receive absolution, and rediscover peace of conscience.

It is a destructive mistake to minimize the importance of the confession of sins in the sacrament of penance. If Christ saw and loved every human person in his passion, took every human sin as his own to the cross and *confessed* every sin, pleading with the Father for forgiveness, his *confession* is undoubtedly the source of the Christian's desire to confess his sins. Among the graces that the Christian obtains from the redemptive death of Jesus is the desire and the ability to acknowledge the sins that so sorely afflicted Christ in his passion, claim responsibility for them, and confess them in order to receive forgiveness. In the confession of sins, the penitent through grace makes Christ's confession of his sins on the cross his own.

Stated simply, when the penitent sincerely and in an integral way confesses sins, he encounters Christ, who suffered for those sins as if he had committed them, confessed them to his Father, and pleaded for their forgiveness. It is Christ, through the Holy Spirit, who empowers the penitent to acknowledge his sins to the priest in order to receive forgiveness and reconciliation with the Father and the Church. In the confession of sins, the Savior's confession on Calvary and the sinner's confession become one. The former confession empowers the latter and elicits forgiveness and healing from the Father.

Simultaneously, the Holy Spirit communicates to the penitent a share in the contrition of the sinless Christ. In the

---

aware of serious sin is reconciled with God and with the church; only physical or moral impossibility excuses the person from confession of this type, in which case reconciliation can take place in other ways."

Second Letter to the Corinthians, Saint Paul tells Christians that there is a sorrow that comes from God:

> You felt a godly grief, so that you suffered no loss through us. For godly grief produces a repentance that leads to salvation and brings no regret, but worldly grief produces death. For see what earnestness this godly grief has produced in you, what eagerness to clear yourselves, what indignation, what alarm, what longing, what zeal, what punishment! (2 Cor 7:9–11)

This supernatural sorrow flows from Christ, the head of the Church, to his members through the action of the Holy Spirit, who gives the penitent an interior participation in the contrition Christ experienced on the Cross. Whether the penitent receives the gift of contrition imperfectly (egocentrically), by grieving for sins out of fear of punishment, or whether he receives it perfectly (selflessly), by mourning sins for the love of God, sacramental absolution causes the penitent to share in Christ's perfect act of contrition, which effects the forgiveness of sins.[14]

---

[14] See Saint Thomas Aquinas, *Summa Theologiae* III, q. 84, a. 1, ad 3. Following his general structure of sacramental causality, Saint Thomas notes that the *sacramentum tantum* (sacramental sign) of penance is made up of both the acts of the penitent (contrition, integral confession, and willingness to make satisfaction) and the absolution of the priest. The *sacramentum et res* (immediate effect of the sacrament) is interior repentance (perfect or imperfect). The absolution of the priest, who represents both Christ and the Church, brings the penitent into saving contact with Christ's passion. This re-presentation, in turn, produces an act of perfect contrition in the penitent with the consequent remission of sins, the *res sacramenti* (grace of the sacrament).

Sacramental theologians should consider the relationship between the priestly power of consecration of the Eucharist and the priestly power of absolution. Might what has often been understood as two distinct powers (or capacities) be in fact one and the same, the second flowing from the first, either reintegrating the sinner into the Eucharistic worship or drawing him more deeply into the Lord's sacrifice?

In absolution, a sacramental act analogous to baptism, Christ justifies and sanctifies the grave sinner through the virtue of his passion and death. To enter into the redeeming act of Christ, the penitent must have sincere sorrow for sins, confess them honestly to the priest, and agree to do penance in expiation for the sins committed. The penance that the priest imposes offers the penitent an opportunity to unite his prayers and sacrifices to Christ's passion for the expiation of sins. The penance reminds the penitent that the sacramental grace of penance, besides the forgiveness of sins, is a renewed and deepened spiritual impulse to live a penitential life.

Saint John Vianney imposed light penances on those who confessed their sins to him. He then did the rest of the penance himself. He admitted to a confrere that he imposed only a small penance on those who confessed their sins properly; the rest he performed in their place. To many priests in the twenty-first century, who are accustomed to perform few or no acts of penance, the practices of Saint John Vianney seem foreign and extreme. The saint understood that his priestly success, his fruitfulness as a confessor, was intrinsically linked to his prayer and acts of penance.

Pope John Paul II, in his Letter to Priests for Holy Thursday of 1986 on Saint John Vianney, masterfully explained that John Vianney chose such a life of extraordinary penance because he recognized that the personal holiness of the pastor affects the receptivity of his people to Christ in the Word and in the sacraments:

> John Mary Vianney sanctified himself so as to be more able to sanctify others. Of course, conversion remains the secret of hearts, which are free in their actions, and the secret of God's grace. By his ministry, the priest can only enlighten people, guide them in the internal forum and give them the sacraments. The sacraments are of course actions of

Christ, and their effectiveness is not diminished by the imperfection or unworthiness of the minister. But the results depend also on the dispositions of those who receive them, and these are greatly assisted by the personal holiness of the priest, by his perceptible witness, as also by the mysterious exchange of merits in the communion of saints. Saint Paul said: "In my flesh I complete what is lacking in Christ's afflictions for the sake of his body, that is, the church." John Mary Vianney in a sense wished to force God to grant these graces of conversion, not only by his prayer but by the sacrifice of his whole life. He wished to love God for those who did not love him, and even to do the penance which they would not do. He was truly a pastor, completely at one with his sinful people.

Hopefully, the 2009–2010 Year for Priests, with its focus on the life and ministry of the Curé of Ars, will inspire priests to discover new forms of penance that will foster pastoral charity. Hopefully, it will also bring a new appreciation of the perennial value of the traditional penitential practices of the Church, namely, prayer, fasting, and almsgiving.

A renewed impetus of prayer and penance among the clergy will surely stimulate a corresponding gospel holiness in the whole Church. Interestingly, John Vianney recognized the absolute need for prayer and penance in his life precisely because he had been empowered by Christ in his ordination to re-present the Paschal Mystery in the absolution of sins and the consecration of the Eucharist. The bishop who ordained him said to John Vianney what the ordaining bishop says to every new priest: "Model your life on the mystery of the Lord's cross."

The penitent's contrition, confession, and satisfaction, inspired by grace, dispose him for the saving intervention of Christ in the sacrament. In absolution, the penitent's contact with the Church, Christ's body, unites him to Christ, the head of the body, in the very act by which he redeemed the members of his Church. Saint Thomas Aquinas' teaching that absolution causes both the contrite and attrite sinner to make an act of perfect contrition for sin becomes luminous in this ecclesial and christological perspective. Through absolution, the penitent enters into Christ's confession of sins, Christ's contrition for sins, and Christ's perfect act of satisfaction for sins. Through the ministry of the Church, the acts of the penitent are mystically transformed by the perfect acts of the crucified Savior. The sinner, passing through the saving passion and death of Christ, participates in Christ's Resurrection through the forgiveness of sins.[15]

During the long hours of hearing confession, Saint John Vianney surely experienced profound union with Christ in his passion, death, and Resurrection. He contemplated, no doubt, how Christ suffered because of the sins of his penitents who confessed to him. The saint pondered, and at times savored, the love of the Savior, who embraces every sinner in his need for forgiveness. He recognized that the

[15] The penitent's therapeutic encounter with Christ in the sacrament may be deeply felt or may be acknowledged solely in the obscurity of faith. The objective salvific encounter of the penitent with Christ does not require or necessarily provoke a manifestation of emotion in the penitent. Because this objective encounter of Christ with a member of his body is so personal and intimate, the strictest seal of secrecy protects the conversation between priest and penitent. The *Catechism of the Catholic Church*, 1467, explains the seal of confession: "Given the delicacy and greatness of this ministry and the respect due to persons, the Church declares that every priest who hears confessions is bound under very severe penalties to keep absolute secrecy regarding the sins that his penitents have confessed to him. He can make no use of knowledge that confession gives him about the penitent's life. This secret, which admits of no exceptions, is called the 'sacramental seal,' because what the penitent has made known to the priest remains 'sealed' by the sacrament."

people who came to him to confess their sins were washed
clean in the blood of Christ through his absolution. He
surely experienced the relief and joy of penitents who were
reconciled through his ministry. Day in and day out, he
witnessed the good Father welcoming back the prodigal son
who had wandered far into the self-destructiveness of sin,
the Good Shepherd lovingly placing the lost sheep on his
shoulders, and the Holy Spirit breathing life into a soul
dead in sin.[16]

Abbé Trochu, in his biography of John Vianney, relates
an incident that took place near the end of the priest's life.
One may imagine that the saint had many similar experiences in the confessional as he witnessed the drama of
redemption played out before his eyes. Mademoiselle Roch,
who reported the event, bears testimony that the Curé of
Ars experienced mystical union with Christ as he heard
confessions. At times, the mystical grace overpowered his
faculties and, outside of the body, he rested in the love of
Christ:

> In 1849 Mlle. Marie Roch, of Paris-Montrouge, came
> to consult M. Vianney. She felt convinced that he alone
> would be able to ease her severe interior trials. After a
> long delay she finally succeeded in getting close to the
> confessional; in fact, she was even able to peer into the

---

[16] The introduction to *The Rite of Penance* (1973) explains the effects of
absolution using the imagery of Scripture: "In the sacrament of penance the
Father receives the repentant son who comes back to him, Christ places the
lost sheep on his shoulders and brings it back to the sheepfold, and the Holy
Spirit sanctifies this temple of God again or lives more fully within it. This
is finally expressed in a renewed and more fervent sharing of the Lord's table,
and there is great joy at the banquet of God's Church over the son who has
returned from afar" (6). As the individual member of the Church is forgiven
and purified in the blood of the Lamb, the entire Church benefits and becomes
resplendent with grace.

dark corner where the saint was seated, and this is what she beheld. The holy priest's face seemed to project two fiery rays, his features being completely hidden by the brightness of their light. But was she not the victim of a hallucination? Yet no delusion appeared possible; she was in perfect possession of her senses, nor could this be a mere play of the sun's light.

As if fascinated by that dazzling countenance, Mlle. Roch gazed at it for at least eight to ten minutes, when it still shone with undimmed radiance. In the end she did not dare to enter the confessional and left the chapel of Saint John the Baptist. But the saint had read in her heart. The next day, after the catechism—that is, about noon—he passed near her. He stopped and said: "Fear nothing, my child, all will be well." [17]

Saint John Vianney reveals to the priest of every age a sacerdotal mysticism rooted objectively in his sacramental ministry and subjectively in his pastoral charity. The saint displayed in his life the ecstatic love of a priest who gives himself totally to Christ in many ways but particularly through the sacraments of penance and the Holy Eucharist. The Curé of Ars prayed faithfully and fervently every day and yearned for even more prayer. His works of penance were constant and intense. Both prayer and penance served his mission of pastoral charity without replacing or obscuring it.

At times, his mission terrified him and made him desire the seclusion of a monastery. More often, the Holy Spirit filled him with wonderful gifts for his penitents, gifts that revealed the real presence of Christ in the priest, and the presence of the priest in Christ. Saint John Vianney was a man of a single motive who burned with the desire to glorify

[17] Abbé Francis Trochu, *The Curé d'Ars: Saint Jean-Marie-Baptiste Vianney*, trans. Dom Ernest Graf, O.S.B. (Rockford, Ill.: TAN Books, 1977), pp. 530–31.

God through pastoral charity. He delighted to be Christ's instrument in healing men wounded by sin. Beyond a doubt, John Vianney was transformed by the grace he administered to souls. Yes, he lived for forty years in the lackluster village of Ars, but in reality, he lived at the very heart of Christ's Paschal Mystery.

9

The Sacred Alliance of the Blessed Virgin and the Priest

Marie Vianney gave her four-year-old son John a small wooden statue of the Blessed Mother. Seventy years later, the Curé of Ars recalled the event: "Oh! how I loved that statue.... Neither by day nor by night would I be parted from it. I should not have slept had I not had it beside me in my little bed.... The Blessed Virgin was the object of my earliest affections; I loved her even before I knew her."[1] His statement indicates that his personal knowledge and love for Mary grew over the years through the grace of the Holy Spirit. Knowledge and love of Mary bespeak an intimate, personal relationship with her.

As his spiritual Mother, the Blessed Virgin had prayed to Christ for John Vianney's vocation to the priesthood. She had nurtured his spiritual life over the years, guarding him from the attacks of the evil one. It was she who had brought him safely to the port of priestly ordination in the face of the many storms he had endured along the way. The saint certainly knew that the Blessed Virgin had been involved in all the good that God had done in him through the years

---

[1] Abbé François Trochu, *The Curé d'Ars: Saint Jean-Marie-Baptiste Vianney*, trans. Dom Ernest Graf, O.S.B. (Rockford, Ill.: TAN Books, 1977), p. 8.

of his preparation for ordination. He knew that she would likewise be involved in all the good that God would accomplish through him as a priest. For this reason, John Vianney dedicated his priesthood to the Mother of God and lived every day in her presence. The Curé of Ars had a childlike relationship with Mary and envisioned her as centrally involved in his priestly ministry. To discuss his daily trials and joys with her was his consolation. Mary was his queen and his Mother, but surely, in the words of Saint Thérèse of Lisieux, she was "more mother than queen". To preach about Mary gave him new life and energy.

On May 1, 1836, John Vianney consecrated his parish to Mary under the title of the Immaculate Conception. Trochu writes, "Shortly afterwards he ordered a heart to be made, in vermeil, which is, even to this day, suspended from the neck of the miraculous Virgin. This heart contains the names of all the parishioners of Ars, written on a white silk ribbon." [2] In 1844 he had another shrine constructed in her honor outside the church. Trochu describes the way the Curé observed Mary's feast days in Ars: "On the feasts of our Lady, Communions were numerous, and the church was never empty. On the evenings of those festivals the nave and the side chapels could barely contain the congregation, for no one wished to miss M. Vianney's homily in honor of our Blessed Lady. The hearers were enthralled by the enthusiasm with which he spoke of the holiness, the power, and the love of the Mother of God." [3] The pastor encouraged every family in Ars to have a statue of the Blessed Virgin on the lawn outside the home and a picture of her over the mantel—signs of consecration of the Curé's flock to her Immaculate Heart.

[2] Ibid., pp. 396–97.
[3] Ibid., p. 397.

Above all other feasts of the Blessed Mother, the Curé of Ars loved the feast of the Immaculate Conception. December 8, 1854, the day of the solemn definition of the dogma of the Immaculate Conception by Blessed Pius IX, was one of the happiest days of his life. Among the many beautiful things he had acquired for his church over the years of his pastorate was a chasuble designed to commemorate the definition of the dogma of the Immaculate Conception. On that day, the Curé of Ars sang the parish Mass in the morning wearing his new chasuble, presided at Vespers in the afternoon, organized a procession through the town, blessed yet another statue of Mary Immaculate, and had the facade of the parish church, the bell tower, and the homes illuminated with floodlights to his delight and that of his parishioners. In the evening, the Curé himself spontaneously rang the church bells for a long time, summoning folk from neighboring villages to Ars to honor Mary. That day the Curé of Ars preached several sermons on the glories of the Mother of God. In the final homily, he said, "What happiness! What happiness! . . . I have always thought that one ray was wanting to the splendour of Catholic dogma: it was a void that had to be filled." [4]

We pause here to consider the role of the Blessed Virgin in both the acquisition and distribution of the grace of the redemption. Mary lived in each of the phases of salvation history—the time before the Messiah, the time during the Messiah's life on earth, and the time after the Messiah's Resurrection—as a servant of his redeeming work. She was so intimately involved in the acquisition of the grace of the redemption because God willed her involvement. As a member of God's Chosen People, Mary yearned and prayed for the coming of the Messiah. God had chosen her, "Daughter Zion",

[4] Ibid., p. 398.

to open the door for the Messiah through her "fiat" and thereby initiate the "fullness of time" (Zech 2:10; Lk 1:38; Gal 4:4). By her consent to God's plan, "the Word became flesh and dwelt among us" (Jn 1:14). It was her flesh and blood, untouched by the sin of Adam, that became his body and blood in the mystery of the Incarnation. Mary welcomed the divine Messiah in the name of her own people and for all people. The Jews and the Gentiles first found him "with Mary his mother" (Mt 2:11; cf. Lk 2:16). She and her spouse, Joseph, nurtured him with love in their home at Nazareth and were the first to marvel at his relationship with his "Abba" in heaven (Lk 2:49–52).

By God's will, the Immaculate Mother of God was Christ's partner in his work of acquiring the grace of redemption for the human family. As recorded in the Gospel of John, Mary hastened and, in a sense, initiated Jesus' public ministry at the wedding at Cana by telling him, "They have no wine" (Jn 2:3). As Christ called and formed disciples, he indicated that his Mother was the perfect disciple who "hear[s] the word of God and do[es] it" (Lk 8:21; cf. Mk 3:35). She is the model for all his disciples.

God willed that Mary accompany her Son to Calvary and share in his suffering through her compassion. At the foot of the Cross, she again consented to the divine will (Jn 19:25–27). The Fathers of the Second Vatican Council described Mary's role in the redeeming sacrifice of Christ:

> The Blessed Virgin advanced in her pilgrimage of faith, and faithfully persevered in her union with her Son unto the cross, where she stood, in keeping with the divine plan, grieving exceedingly with her only begotten Son, uniting herself with a maternal heart with His sacrifice, and lovingly consenting to the immolation of this Victim which she herself had brought forth. Finally, she was

given by the same Christ Jesus dying on the cross as a mother to His disciple with these words: "Woman, behold thy son". (*Lumen Gentium*, 58)

The Fathers of Vatican II also explain precisely how Mary participated in Christ's passion and made her unique contribution to our redemption, becoming our Mother in the realm of sanctifying grace: "She was united with Him by compassion as He died on the Cross. In this wholly singular way she cooperated by her obedience, faith, hope and burning charity in the work of the Savior in giving back supernatural life to souls. Wherefore she is our mother in the order of grace" (61).

With the apostles and the other disciples, Mary enjoyed the presence of the risen Christ and remained with the disciples in the Upper Room after his ascension into heaven, praying for the coming of the promised Holy Spirit (Acts 1:12–24). After Pentecost, she accompanied the neophyte Church as the privileged witness to the Incarnation and the spiritual Mother of all believers. As she had joined the people of Israel in praying for the coming of the Messiah, so she now joined her voice to that of the new Israel, the Church, in pleading for his return in glory.

At the end of her earthly life, Mary was assumed bodily into heaven. Beholding the face of God, she joins in Christ's intercession for the salvation of all people. In heaven, Our Lady continues her saving mission as spiritual Mother of the faithful. We turn once more to the Fathers of the Second Vatican Council to receive their teaching on Mary's role as mediatrix of grace:

Taken up to heaven she did not lay aside this salvific duty, but by her constant intercession continued to bring us the gifts of eternal salvation. By her maternal charity,

she cares for the brethren of her Son, who still journey
on earth surrounded by dangers and difficulties, until they
are led into the happiness of their true home. Therefore
the Blessed Virgin is invoked by the Church under the
titles of Advocate, Auxiliatrix, Adjutrix, and Mediatrix.
(*Lumen Gentium*, 62)

Because God willed and continues to will the personal
involvement of the Mother of God in the mystery of salvation, it is essential for the priest, the minister of salvation,
to understand and appreciate her place in his life. Stated in
the simplest possible way, Mary obtains every priest's vocation through her intercession. Then, in a mysterious way,
she is intimately involved in the reception of that grace,
opening the "ears of the heart" to hear and respond to the
call of Christ. As the seminarian's spiritual Mother, Mary
serves the Holy Spirit in preparing the candidate to receive
the character of the sacrament of holy orders. After ordination, the priest who intentionally entrusts his concerns
and good works to her care discovers in her a mysterious
source of spiritual discernment and fruitfulness.

There are many similarities in the devotion to Our Lady
of Saint John Vianney and Saint Louis-Marie de Montfort
(1673–1716), the author of *True Devotion to Mary*.[5] One might
say that de Montfort and Vianney are two sons of the same
Mother, each raised in the French school of spirituality. Saint
John Vianney's teaching on Our Lady in his Catechism[6]
surely reflects the thought of the saint from Montfort: "When
our hands have touched spices, they give fragrance to all

---

[5] Saint Louis de Montfort, *True Devotion to Mary* (Bay Shore, NY: Montfort Publications, 1980).
[6] *The Little Catechism of the Curé of Ars* (Rockford, Ill.: TAN Books, 1986),
p. 17.

they handle. Let us make our prayers pass through the hands of the Blessed Virgin. She will make them fragrant."

Saint Louis de Montfort, in encouraging consecration to Mary, calls the seminarian[7] or priest to stand at the foot of Jesus' Cross and receive Mary as his parting gift, "taking her into his home", that is, into a deep, filial relationship. The consecration prepares him to give Christ everything through her. *Everything* means his present and future, his body and soul, all his material possessions, and the value of every spiritual gift. Consecration to Mary according to de Montfort is nothing less than the total abandonment of self to Christ through Mary for the sake of the Church, a program for an entire lifetime of priestly service. Its aim is to

[7] Saint Louis de Montfort's *True Devotion to Mary* is an excellent tool for the formation of future priests. The saint from Montfort certainly has the knack of forming priests who have a devotion to Mary like the Curé of Ars! It should be noted that priestly formation in this spirituality is incomplete apart from solid intellectual formation in the Marian doctrine of the Church in the classroom, practices of devotion to Mary as part of the daily schedule in the seminary, and the example of the seminary formators' devotion to Mary. Consecration to Mary for the seminarian involves entrustment of every facet of his discernment and formation to Mary's care. The seminarians are formed in this spirituality in the external forum through conferences given by the rector or director of spiritual formation and, in the internal forum, by the seminarian's personal spiritual guide. The seminary helps to instill in the future priest Jesus' love for his Mother and to help him understand that Mary truly gives birth to Christ's life in souls and nurtures that life.

See also *Lumen Gentium*, 60: "There is but one Mediator as we know from the words of the apostle, 'for there is one God and one mediator of God and men, the man Christ Jesus, who gave himself as redemption for all'. The maternal duty of Mary toward men in no wise obscures or diminishes this unique mediation of Christ, but rather shows His power. For all the salvific influence of the Blessed Virgin on men originates, not from some inner necessity, but from the divine pleasure. It flows forth from the superabundance of the merits of Christ, rests on His mediation, depends entirely on it and draws all its power from it. In no way does it impede, but rather does it foster the immediate union of the faithful with Christ."

build in the priest that abandonment to the Father's will that both Jesus and Mary exhibited on Calvary—Christ as redeemer and Mary as the first and most perfect recipient of the grace of redemption.

For the priest, consecration to Mary involves entrustment of every facet of priestly life and ministry to her care. The priest invites the Blessed Mother to accompany him in the celebration of the liturgy and the administration of the sacraments; in his personal communion with the Father, the Son, and the Holy Spirit in personal prayer; and in the pastoral service he gives to the people of God. He depends on the help of Mary's prayers to die to self in obeying the will of God manifested through his bishop. He seeks Mary's poverty of spirit in all that is involved in the faithful observance of celibacy and simplicity of life.

Often, at a given point or points in his life, a priest feels the need to do more for God, to be more generous and sacrificial. This movement of grace takes either the form of a disturbing recognition of mediocrity in living the priestly life or a yearning for deeper union with God. The consecration to Mary of de Montfort provides a way for the priest to respond to this grace and deepen his self-oblation to Christ with the maternal help of Mary. Many priests are convinced that consecration to Mary has changed their lives for the better.

Since each priest has been asked by Christ to take Mary "into his home" (cf. Jn 19:25–27), that is, into the heart of his ministerial priesthood,[8] he has the joy of loving her as

---

[8] In his Letter to Priests for Holy Thursday of 1988 on the Blessed Virgin Mary in the life of the priest, Pope John Paul II noted that although the disciple at the foot of the cross (Jn 19:25–27) represents all disciples, he is nonetheless also a priest. Consequently, Our Lord asks him to take Mary and all that is inscribed in her heart into the "home" of his ministerial priesthood.

his own Mother as well as the responsibility of encouraging love and devotion to Mary among the people of God. The lay faithful are blessed when their pastors teach them to have a filial relationship with Jesus' Mother, their Mother. Saint Louis de Montfort's *True Devotion to Mary* is a tool at hand for the accomplishment of this good work of the priest.

Just as Mary's involvement in the acquisition of the grace of the redemption was necessary because God willed her intimate union with Christ, so her involvement in the distribution of the grace of the redemption is necessary also because God wills it until the end of the ages. The title of this chapter mentions the "sacred alliance" of Mary and the priest. Let us look more closely at this mystery: In heaven, Mary shares in her Son's universal salvific will (1 Tim 2:4). With him, she prays that all people will be saved by receiving his grace to turn away from sin and enter into a loving relationship with the Trinity.

According to God's plan of salvation, the grace of the redemption is distributed through the prayer, sacrifices, and suffering of the Church, Christ's body on earth. To be specific, the grace of the objective redemption is offered and applied to souls subjectively through the preaching of the Word of God, through the administration of the sacraments of the Church—especially the re-presentation of the sacrifice of the Cross in the Holy Eucharist—and through pastoral charity in all of its manifestations. Priests are commissioned by Christ to preach, to administer the grace of the redemption through the sacraments, and to shepherd God's people. Therefore, Mary's heavenly desires—in reality, Christ's heavenly desires—to bring all to salvation are ordinarily accomplished through the ministry of priests.

Here is the sacred alliance! Mary has a special concern for priests and an interest in their work since they are the

channels of the grace of her Son's redemptive sacrifice. We
may say that Mary is particularly concerned with the sanctification of her priest sons since the salvation of so many
other people depends on them. Conversely, priests have the
powerful presence and supreme intercession of Mary at their
disposal. Together, and only together, will they, Mary and
the priest, bring all men to Christ in faith and love. Consecration to Mary makes the priest's ontological alliance with
her conscious and intentional. It unites him in a special
way to the intentions of her heart.

It is not Mary's mission to preach the gospel, or administer the sacraments, or govern the Church. Her role is to
accompany those who share in the mission of her Son as
priests and make their work fruitful through her motherly
intercession in heaven. As their spiritual Mother, Mary also
accompanies those who hear the Word and receive the sacraments. As Christ's first disciple, Mary shows her children
what it means to hear and surrender to the Word of God.
As the one who has given the perfect response of love to
God's Word, she helps her children respond in kind. In and
through the Church, Mary mysteriously gives birth to Christ
in the souls of her children in baptism. When they wound
themselves through sin, the *Immaculata* helps her sons and
daughters confess their sins in sacramental penance. She disposes them to receive Jesus in Holy Communion as she
received him in the mystery of the Incarnation. Her motherly love for her children draws them to deeper communion with Christ, filling them with that holiness that is the
beginning of eternal life. Mary is truly the Mother of Divine
Grace, the Mother of the Church.

This brings us back to our saint's delight in the mystery
of the Immaculate Conception: Did John Vianney rejoice
so ecstatically on the day of the definition of the dogma

because he realized that the same sovereign grace of God that had preserved Mary from sin from the moment of her conception had been at work liberating his penitents from the sins they confessed to him? Perhaps on December 8, 1854, the Curé of Ars understood as never before the sacred alliance that exists between the priest and the Mother of God in the distribution of the grace of redemption. Mary prayed for John Vianney's vocation. Jesus made him his priest. Mary prayed for a special sanctification of the Curé of Ars. Jesus made him holy. Mary prayed for all the charisms necessary for the phenomenon of Ars. Jesus poured them into Vianney's soul. Mary prayed for the conversion of sinners. Jesus drew them, through the Holy Spirit, to the Curé's confessional. Vianney's willingness to be the humble instrument of Christ's charity reveals the presence of Mary's maternal mediation.

On occasions, the sacred alliance of the Mother of God and Saint John Vianney became visible and, to an extent, public. Among those who gave testimony at the processes for the beatification and canonization of the Curé of Ars were those who actually saw and heard him speaking to the Blessed Virgin present in his room. This seems to have been a regular occurrence. One of his collaborators in the works of charity, Mademoiselle Étiennette Durié, related this incident that took place on May 8, 1840, eighteen years before the apparitions of the Blessed Virgin to Saint Bernadette in Lourdes:

> One o'clock had just struck. M. Vianney was alone in his room, and Catherine Lassagne let me into the presbytery. As I was going up the staircase, I heard M. Vianney's voice as if he were in conversation with someone, so I went up softly and listened. Someone said to him in a very gentle tone of voice: "What do you ask?"

"Ah! my good Mother, I ask for the conversion of sinners, the comfort of those in affliction, the relief of my sick people, especially that of one who has long been suffering and pleads either for death or a cure."

"She will get well," the voice replied, "but a little later."

On hearing these words I hurried into the room, the door of which had remained ajar. I was suffering from cancer, and felt sure that I was the person under discussion. What was my astonishment on beholding, standing in front of the fire-place, a lady of ordinary stature, clad in a robe of dazzling whiteness, on which were scattered golden roses. Her shoes appeared to be as white as snow. On her fingers shone the brightest of diamonds, and around her head was a wreath of stars which flashed like the sun, so that I was dazzled by their brilliance.

When at last I felt able to raise my eyes to her once more, I saw her smile gently. "My good Mother," I exclaimed, "do take me with you to Heaven!"

"Later on."

"Ah! Now is the time, Mother!"

"You will always be my child, and I shall always be a mother to you." After uttering these words she disappeared. For a while I remained dumbfounded, for I was overcome at the thought that such a grace should have been vouchsafed to me. "Is it possible to witness such wonderful things and yet remain so ungrateful?" I said to myself. When I came to, I noticed M. le Curé still standing at his table, with his hands joined on his breast, his countenance radiant, and his gaze fixed. I feared that he was dead, so I approached and pulled at his cassock. "My God, is it you?" he said.

"No, Father, it is I." And as I uttered the words he came to himself and made a movement. "Where were you, Father? What have you seen?"

"I have seen a lady."

"So have I; who is this lady?"

"If you speak of it," M. Vianney said severely, "you shall never again set foot in this room."

"Shall I tell you what I thought, Father? I thought it was our Lady."

"And you were not mistaken ... So you have seen her?" [9]

Why Étiennette Durié was invited by God to enter into the Curé's conversation with the Mother of God is unknown. It is significant that his first prayer was for the conversion of sinners, his second for the health of the sick. This episode, which is far from unique in the life of the saint, helps us understand the intimacy of the Curé of Ars and our Blessed Mother. It exemplifies the intimacy every priest should have with Mary. Saint John Vianney's sacred alliance with Mary in the mystery of her Immaculate Conception was the source of his priestly fruitfulness. It explains the zeal, fortitude, and gentleness he displayed in his ministry of reconciliation. The saint's covenant with Mary is surely at the heart of the "grace of Ars".

[9] Trochu, *Curé d'Ars*, pp. 531–33.

10

Saint John Vianney:
Icon of the Divine Bridegroom
of the Church

Not far from Ars, a drive of about two hours along beautiful country roads, is the mountain town of Paray-le-Monial. Arriving in the center of the town, one is drawn to the beautiful tenth- or eleventh-century Romanesque basilica where once the abbots of Cluny spent their summers. Some come to Paray-le-Monial to visit the beautiful basilica, stroll through the well-preserved medieval village, and enjoy the artistic treasures and the rich wines of Burgundy. Most come for a different reason.

A short distance down the road from the basilica is a convent of Visitation Nuns, the daughters of Saint Francis de Sales and Saint Jane Frances de Chantal. Here in 1673–1674 Jesus Christ appeared on at least four occasions to another "little one of God", Saint Margaret Mary Alacoque. He brought her a lament: "Love is not loved." Christ showed Margaret Mary his wounded heart. She experienced the love that burned in his heart for his Father and for every human being as he hung on the Cross. She *saw* the piercing of the Lord's heart on Calvary and *felt* his thirst for the love of those he redeemed. Our Lord shared with her his desires for the affection of all men. He expressed his desire for the conversion of sinners. Jesus asked Margaret Mary to tell everyone about his Sacred Heart. Calling all to the Eucharist, he requested reparation. He promised special graces to those who would honor his heart.

The Jesuit Saint Claude la Colombière helped Margaret Mary understand Jesus' requests. Together, as Jesus' servants, they overcame the many obstacles that stood in the way of the propagation of the devotion. In the process, they suffered for Christ and with Christ. In the end, Jesus conquered, and the devotion to his Sacred Heart spread throughout the Church in France and the Church universal.

Saint John Vianney knew of the apparitions of the Sacred Heart. He understood that devotion to the Eucharistic Heart of Christ is the Church's premier act of love. Placing an image of the Sacred Heart of Jesus in a prominent place in the parish church, he encouraged his people to have confidence in the Heart of Christ. The Curé of Ars himself loved the Sacred Heart and promoted devotion far and wide.

When Christ appeared to Saint Margaret Mary, he told her of the many graces that would come to all who honor his Sacred Heart. It is beneficial to recall the twelve promises that Christ made to all Christians devoted to his Heart. Surely, these promises were fulfilled powerfully in the life and priestly ministry of the Curé of Ars:

1. I will give them all the graces necessary in their state of life.
2. I will establish peace in their families.
3. I will console them in all their difficulties.
4. I will be their secure refuge during life and especially at the hour of death.
5. I will bestow abundant blessings upon all their undertakings.

6. Sinners shall find in My Heart the source and infinite ocean of mercy.

7. Tepid souls shall grow fervent.

8. Fervent souls shall quickly grow to high perfection.

9. I will bless every place in which a picture of My Heart shall be exposed and honored.

10. *I will give to priests the gift of touching the most hardened hearts.*

11. Those who promote this devotion shall have their names written in My Heart, never to be blotted out.

12. I promise in the excessive mercy of My Heart that My all-powerful love will grant to all those who communicate on the First Friday in nine consecutive months the grace of final penitence; they shall not die in My displeasure nor without receiving the Sacraments; My Divine Heart shall be their safe refuge in the last moment.[1]

One may only wonder how much of Saint John Vianney's spiritual success in the confessional was the result, the fruit, of his devotion to the Sacred Heart of Jesus. Without a doubt, this devotion is another facet of the grace of Ars. Father Vianney had the special grace promised to priests who have and spread devotion to the heart of Christ: "I will give to priests the gift of touching the most hardened hearts."

All of the priests and seminarians I know who have made a pilgrimage to Ars and Paray-le-Monial returned home

---

[1] Priests of the Sacred Heart, *Daily Prayers* (Hales Corners, Wis.: Priests of the Sacred Heart, n.d.), inside front cover. Emphasis added.

with either a new or renewed devotion to the Heart of Christ and a desire to spread the devotion among the faithful. This devotion to the Sacred Heart increases their desire to bring people back to Christ through the sacraments. This, I am convinced, is one of the graces of the pilgrimage.

Whenever I visit Ars and Paray-le-Monial, I am struck by the one spirit that permeates both of these holy places. In each sanctuary there is the manifestation of the ardent love of the Heart of Christ for all people—and especially for those who are farthest away from him and his love. There is the spirit of prayer, penance, and reparation; a love for the Eucharist and the sacrament of reconciliation; and a profound reverence for the priest as another Christ. There is a sense of the maternal presence of the Mother of God. In both places there are many signs of vitality and health—many seminarians, young religious men and women, families with lots of children, and many members of various ecclesial movements.

If you have the good fortune to make a retreat in Ars, I recommend that you conclude the retreat with a pilgrimage to Paray-le-Monial. Try to spend at least a whole day there. If you are a priest, arrange to offer Holy Mass in the chapel of the Visitation convent where Jesus revealed his heart to Saint Margaret Mary. The Blessed Sacrament is often solemnly exposed in the chapel. Spend as much time there as you can. Contemplate the love in the heart of Jesus for you and for all people. Feel Christ's thirst for the love of those who are alienated from him by sin.

In my experience, the grace of Ars manifests itself with a mystical fullness in Paray-le-Monial. Perhaps it is the simple recognition that the Heart of Jesus is revealed in the love of the Curé of Ars. In a mysterious, wonderful way, Ars and Paray-le-Monial are intimately related. One casts

light on the other. Jesus revealed his Heart in all of its splendor to Saint Margaret Mary in Paray-le-Monial. Jesus again
bared his Heart in the daily and ordinary life of the pastor
of Ars. How often John Vianney said, "The priest continues the work of redemption on earth. . . . If we really understood the priest on earth, we would die not of fright but of
love. . . . The Priesthood is the love of the heart of Jesus." [2]

In naming Saint John Vianney the patron saint of all priests,
Pope Benedict XVI has cast a brilliant light on the spirituality of all who participate in the priesthood of Christ
through the sacrament of holy orders. Although the spiritual emphasis of one or another of the religious orders may
indeed help a priest in his pursuit of Christian holiness, all
priests have a spirituality that is more ancient than that of
any order in the Church. Priestly spirituality flows from
the apostles' participation in the priestly holiness and mission of Jesus himself. John Vianney understood this and therefore said so often in his preaching and catechesis, "The
Priesthood is the love of the heart of Jesus."

This love is manifested in the priest's intercession for the
salvation of all people, in his zeal to bring Christ to every
person who does not know or love him, in preaching the
gospel and teaching the Catholic faith, in the celebration
of the Mass and the sacraments, and in pastoral concern for
all God's people—especially those who are poor and unloved.

Through the character and grace of holy orders, the priest
shares the pastoral charity of the Good Shepherd. Only by
allowing Christ the Priest to live and act in him may the
priest become holy. Even the monk or hermit who is a
priest can become holy through pastoral love for the flock
of Christ. The monk's or hermit's Mass and his hidden prayer

[2] *Catechism of the Catholic Church*, 1589.

and penances energize those priests who serve the people in the parishes and other apostolates of the Church. His hidden priestly service disposes the people to receive the Word of God and the grace of the sacraments.

The humble Curé of Ars is the model of priestly holiness for all who bear the glorious seal of Jesus' priesthood and the grace of holy orders in their souls. His life beckons all priests to work assiduously during the Year for Priests and beyond to restore and deepen the practice of frequent confession in the life of the Church for the sake of the Heart of Christ truly present in the Holy Eucharist and to build a Church and society permeated by the values of Christ's gospel.

After John Vianney's death, a woman who lived in a neighboring village wrote a letter to the new parish priest of Ars in which she described an incident she experienced when meeting with the Curé of Ars:

> I deem it a duty to inform you that I was at Ars on July 2, 1856, and not having succeeded in seeing the saint in the confessional, owing to the crowd of strangers that thronged round it, I promised myself the satisfaction of at least throwing myself at his feet to ask for his blessing. As soon, therefore, as I came into the presence of that wonderful man, I endeavoured to grasp his sacred hand so as to kiss it reverently. But he withdrew it, saying to me in a grave yet gracious manner: "Oh! Do not rob me of my ring!"
>
> At that same moment, I saw what I had not noticed until then: on the fourth finger of his left hand there shone a golden ring of extraordinary brilliancy.[3]

[3] Abbé François Trochu, *The Curé d'Ars: Saint Jean-Marie-Baptiste Vianney*, trans. Dom Ernest Graf, O.S.B. (Rockford, Ill.: TAN Books, 1977), pp. 544-45.

Some have seen in this mystic ring an indication of the transforming union, the perfection of the spiritual life, as described by Saint Teresa of Avila in *The Interior Castle*. Spiritual authors have seen Vianney's ring as a sign of the highest development of the life of charity that a person may attain in this life—a kind of marriage of the soul with Christ. Without denying in any way that the Curé of Ars had reached these heights of sanctity, I dare to propose another explanation of this "golden ring of extraordinary brilliancy" in light of the Curé's pastoral love for Christ's flock.

Might the marriage band not indicate the perfect configuration of the Curé of Ars to Christ, the head and bridegroom of the Church who "loved the Church and gave himself up for her, that he might sanctify her, having cleansed her by the washing of water with the word, that he might present the Church to himself in splendor, without spot or wrinkle or any such thing, that she might be holy and without blemish" (Eph 5:25–27)? Might it be the symbol of the presence of the love of the heart of Christ in the poor, human heart of a priest, a token that the God who is love will never abandon his people? Might the ring be the sign of John Vianney's spiritual marriage to the Church that produced scores of sons and daughters for the Kingdom of heaven?

It is good to bring our pilgrimage to Ars to an end by inviting the Curé of Ars to give us a simple catechetical lesson on the grace of Ars.

My children, we have come to the Sacrament of Orders. It is a Sacrament which seems to relate to no one among you, and which yet relates to every one. This Sacrament raises man up to God. What is a priest? A man who holds the place of God—a man who is invested with all the powers of God. "Go," said our Lord to the priest; "as my Father sent Me, I send you. All power has been given Me in heaven and on earth. Go then, teach all nations. . . . He who listens to you, listens to Me; he who despises you, despises Me." When the priest remits sins, he does not say, "God pardons you;" he says, "I absolve you." At the Consecration, he does not say, "This is the Body of our Lord;" he says, "This is My Body."

Saint Bernard tells us that every thing has come to us through Mary; and we may also say that every thing has come to us through the priest; yes, all happiness, all graces, all heavenly gifts.

If we had not the Sacrament of Orders, we should not have our Lord. Who placed Him there, in that tabernacle? It was the priest. Who was it that received your soul, on its entrance into life? The priest. Who nourishes it, to give it strength to make its pilgrimage? The priest. Who will prepare it to appear before God, by washing that soul, for the last time, in the Blood of Jesus Christ? The priest—always the priest. And if that soul comes to the point of death, who will raise it up, who will restore it to calmness and peace? Again, the priest. You cannot recall one single blessing from God without finding, side by side with this recollection, the image of the priest.

Go to confession to the Blessed Virgin, or to an angel; will they absolve you? No. Will they give you the Body and Blood of our Lord? No. The Holy Virgin cannot make her Divine Son descend into the Host. You might have two hundred angels there, but they could not absolve you. A priest, however simple he may be, can do it; he can say to you, "Go in peace; I pardon you."

Oh, how great is a priest! The priest will not understand the greatness of his office till he is in heaven. If he understood it on earth, he would die, not of fear, but of love.

The other benefits of God would be of no avail to us without the priest. What would be the use of a house full of gold, if you had nobody to open you the door? The priest has the key of the heavenly treasures; it is he who opens the door; he is the steward of the good God, the distributor of His wealth.

Without the priest, the Death and Passion of our Lord would be of no avail. Look at the heathens: what has it availed them that our Lord has died? Alas! they can have no share in the blessings of redemption, while they have no priests to apply His Blood to their souls!

The priest is not a priest for himself; he does not give himself absolution; he does not administer the Sacraments to himself. He is not for himself, he is for you.

After God, the priest is every thing. Leave a parish twenty years without priests; they will worship beasts.

If the Missionary Father and I were to go away, you would say, "What can we do in this church? there is no Mass; our Lord is no longer there: we may as well pray at home." When people wish to destroy religion, they begin by attacking the priest, because where there is no longer any priest there is no sacrifice, and where there is no longer any sacrifice there is no religion.

When the bell calls you to church, if you were asked, "Where are you going?" you might answer, "I am going to feed my soul." If someone were to ask you, pointing to the tabernacle, "What is that golden door?" "That is our storehouse, where the true Food of our souls is kept." "Who has the key? Who lays in the provisions? Who makes ready the feast, and who serves the table?" "The priest." "And what is the Food?" "The precious Body and Blood of our Lord." O God! O God! how Thou hast loved us! . . .

See the power of the priest; out of a piece of bread the word of a priest makes a God. It is more than creating the world.... Some one said, "Does St. Philomena, then, obey the Curé of Ars?" Indeed, she may well obey him, since God obeys him.

If I were to meet a priest and an angel, I should salute the priest before I saluted the angel. The latter is the friend of God; but the priest holds His place. St. Teresa kissed the ground where a priest had passed. When you see a priest, you should say, "There is he who made me a child of God, and opened heaven to me by holy Baptism; he who purified me after I had sinned; who gives nourishment to my soul." At the sight of a church-tower, you may say, "What is there in that place?" "The Body of our Lord." "Why is He there?" "Because a priest has been there, and has said holy Mass."

What joy did the Apostles feel after the Resurrection of our Lord, at seeing the Master whom they had loved so much! The priest must feel the same joy, at seeing our Lord whom he holds in his hands. Great value is attached to objects which have been laid in the drinking-cup of the Blessed Virgin and of the Child Jesus, at Loretto. But the fingers of the priest, that have touched the adorable Flesh of Jesus Christ, that have been plunged into the chalice which contained His Blood, into the pyx where His Body has lain, are they not still more precious?

The priesthood is the love of the Heart of Jesus. When you see the priest, think of our Lord Jesus Christ.[4]

The priest continues the work of redemption on earth.

If we really understood the priest on earth, we would die not of fright but of love.

The priesthood is the love of the Heart of Jesus.

---

[4] Saint John Vianney, "Catechism on the Priesthood", in *The Spirit of the Curé of Ars*, trans. Abbé Monnin, ed. John Edward Bowden (London: Burns, Lambert, and Oates, 1865), pp. 69–73.

APPENDICES

I

Letter of His Holiness
Pope Benedict XVI
Proclaiming a Year for Priests on the
150th Anniversary of the "Dies Natalis"
of the Curé of Ars

Dear Brother Priests,

On the forthcoming Solemnity of the Most Sacred Heart of Jesus, Friday 19 June 2009—a day traditionally devoted to prayer for the sanctification of the clergy—, I have decided to inaugurate a "Year for Priests" in celebration of the 150th anniversary of the *"dies natalis"* of John Mary Vianney, the patron saint of parish priests worldwide.[1] This Year, meant to deepen the commitment of all priests to interior renewal for the sake of a stronger and more incisive witness to the Gospel in today's world, will conclude on the same Solemnity in 2010. *"The priesthood is the love of the heart of Jesus"*, the saintly Curé of Ars would often say.[2] This touching expression makes us reflect, first of all, with heartfelt gratitude on the immense gift which priests represent, not only for the Church, but also

[1] He was proclaimed as such by Pope Pius XI in 1929.

[2] *"Le Sacerdoce, c'est l'amour du cœur de Jésus"* (in *Le curé d'Ars: Sa pensée—Son cœur.* Présentés par l'Abbé Bernard Nodet, éd. Xavier Mappus [Foi Vivante, 1966], p. 98). Hereafter: *Nodet.* The expression is also quoted in the *Catechism of the Catholic Church,* no. 1589.

for humanity itself. I think of all those priests who quietly present Christ's words and actions each day to the faithful and to the whole world, striving to be one with the Lord in their thoughts and their will, their sentiments and their style of life. How can I not pay tribute to their apostolic labours, their tireless and hidden service, their universal charity? And how can I not praise the courageous fidelity of so many priests who, even amid difficulties and incomprehension, remain faithful to their vocation as "friends of Christ", whom he has called by name, chosen and sent?

I still treasure the memory of the first parish priest at whose side I exercised my ministry as a young priest: he left me an example of unreserved devotion to his pastoral duties, even to meeting his own death in the act of bringing viaticum to a gravely ill person. I also recall the countless confreres whom I have met and continue to meet, not least in my pastoral visits to different countries, men generously dedicated to the daily exercise of their priestly ministry. Yet the expression of Saint John Mary also makes us think of Christ's pierced Heart and the crown of thorns which surrounds it. I also think, therefore, of the countless situations of suffering endured by many priests, either because they themselves share in the manifold human experience of pain or because they encounter misunderstanding from the very persons to whom they minister. How can we not also think of all those priests who are offended in their dignity, obstructed in their mission and persecuted, even at times to offering the supreme testimony of their own blood?

There are also, sad to say, situations which can never be sufficiently deplored where the Church herself suffers as a consequence of infidelity on the part of some of her ministers. Then it is the world which finds grounds for scandal and rejection. What is most helpful to the Church in such cases is not only a frank and complete acknowledgment of the weaknesses of her ministers, but also a joyful and renewed realization of the greatness of God's gift, embodied in the splendid example of generous pastors, religious afire with love for God and for souls, and insightful, patient spiritual guides. Here the teaching and example of Saint John Mary Vianney can serve as a significant point of reference for us all. The Curé of Ars was very humble, yet as a priest he was conscious of being an immense gift to his people: "A good shepherd, a pastor after God's heart, is the greatest treasure which the good Lord can grant to a parish, and one of the most precious gifts of divine mercy." [3] He spoke of the priesthood as if incapable of fathoming the grandeur of the *gift* and *task* entrusted to a human creature: "O, how great is the priest! ... If he realized what he is, he would die.... God obeys him: he utters a few words and the Lord descends from heaven at his voice, to be contained within a small host...." [4] Explaining to his parishioners the importance of the sacraments, he would say: "Without the Sacrament of Holy Orders, we would not have the Lord. Who put him there in that tabernacle? The priest. Who welcomed your soul at the beginning of your life? The priest. Who feeds your soul and gives it strength for its journey? The priest. Who will prepare it to appear before God, bathing it one last time in the blood of Jesus Christ? The priest, always the priest. And if this soul should happen to die [as a result of sin], who will raise it up, who will restore its calm and peace? Again, the priest.... After God, the priest is everything! ... Only in heaven will he fully realize what he is." [5] These words, welling up from the priestly heart of

---

[3] Nodet, p. 101.

[4] Ibid., p. 97.

[5] Ibid., pp. 98–99.

the holy pastor, might sound excessive. Yet they reveal the
high esteem in which he held the sacrament of the priesthood. He seemed overwhelmed by a boundless sense of
responsibility: "Were we to fully realize what a priest is on
earth, we would die: not of fright, but of love.... Without
the priest, the passion and death of our Lord would be of
no avail. It is the priest who continues the work of redemption on earth.... What use would be a house filled with
gold, were there no one to open its door? The priest holds
the key to the treasures of heaven: it is he who opens the
door: he is the steward of the good Lord; the administrator
of his goods.... Leave a parish for twenty years without a
priest, and they will end by worshiping the beasts there....
The priest is not a priest for himself, he is a priest for you." [6]

He arrived in Ars, a village of 230 souls, warned by his
Bishop beforehand that there he would find religious practice in a sorry state: "There is little love of God in that
parish; you will be the one to put it there." As a result, he
was deeply aware that he needed to go there to embody
Christ's presence and to bear witness to his saving mercy:
"[Lord,] grant me the conversion of my parish; I am willing to suffer whatever you wish, for my entire life!": with
this prayer he entered upon his mission.[7] The Curé devoted
himself completely to his parish's conversion, setting before
all else the Christian education of the people in his care.
Dear brother priests, let us ask the Lord Jesus for the grace
to learn for ourselves something of the pastoral plan of Saint
John Mary Vianney! The first thing we need to learn is the
complete identification of the man with his ministry. In
Jesus, person and mission tend to coincide: all Christ's saving

[6] Ibid., pp. 98–100.
[7] Ibid., p. 183.

activity was, and is, an expression of his "filial consciousness" which from all eternity stands before the Father in an
attitude of loving submission to his will. In a humble yet
genuine way, every priest must aim for a similar identification. Certainly this is not to forget that the efficacy of the
ministry is independent of the holiness of the minister; but
neither can we overlook the extraordinary fruitfulness of
the encounter between the ministry's objective holiness and
the subjective holiness of the minister. The Curé of Ars
immediately set about this patient and humble task of har-
monizing his life as a minister with the holiness of the ministry he had received, by deciding to "*live*", physically, in
his parish church: As his first biographer tells us: "Upon his
arrival, he chose the church as his home. He entered the
church before dawn and did not leave it until after the evening Angelus. There he was to be sought whenever
needed." [8]

The pious excess of his devout biographer should not
blind us to the fact that the Curé also knew how to "live"
actively within the entire territory of his parish: he regularly visited the sick and families, organized popular missions and patronal feasts, collected and managed funds for
charitable and missionary works, embellished and furnished
his parish church, cared for the orphans and teachers of the
"*Providence*" (an institute he founded); provided for the education of children; founded confraternities and enlisted lay
persons to work at his side.

His example naturally leads me to point out that there
are sectors of cooperation which need to be opened ever
more fully to the lay faithful. Priests and laity together make

[8] Monnin, A., *Il Curato d'Ars: Vita di Gian.Battista-Maria Vianney*, vol. I,
ed. Marietti [Turin, 1870], p. 122.

up the one priestly people[9] and in virtue of their ministry priests live in the midst of the lay faithful, "that they may lead everyone to the unity of charity, 'loving one another with mutual affection; and outdoing one another in sharing honour'" (Rom 12:10).[10] Here we ought to recall the Second Vatican Council's hearty encouragement to priests "to be sincere in their appreciation and promotion of the dignity of the laity and of the special role they have to play in the Church's mission.... They should be willing to listen to lay people, give brotherly consideration to their wishes, and acknowledge their experience and competence in the different fields of human activity. In this way they will be able together with them to discern the signs of the times."[11]

Saint John Mary Vianney taught his parishioners primarily by the witness of his life. It was from his example that they learned to pray, halting frequently before the tabernacle for a visit to Jesus in the Blessed Sacrament.[12] "One need not say much to pray well"—the Curé explained to them—"We know that Jesus is there in the tabernacle: let us open our hearts to him, let us rejoice in his sacred presence. That is the best prayer."[13] And he would urge them: "Come to communion, my brothers and sisters, come to Jesus. Come to live from him in order to live with him...."[14] "Of course you are not worthy of him, but *you need him!*"[15]

[9] Cf. *Lumen Gentium*, 10.

[10] Presbyterorum Ordinis, 9.

[11] Ibid.

[12] "Contemplation is a gaze of faith, fixed on Jesus. 'I look at him and he looks at me': this is what a certain peasant of Ars used to say to his holy Curé about his prayer before the tabernacle" (*Catechism of the Catholic Church*, no. 2715).

[13] Nodet, p. 85.

[14] Ibid., p. 114.

[15] Ibid., p. 119.

This way of educating the faithful *to the Eucharistic presence and to communion* proved most effective when they saw him celebrate the Holy Sacrifice of the Mass. Those present said that "it was not possible to find a finer example of worship. . . . He gazed upon the Host with immense love." [16] "All good works, taken together, do not equal the sacrifice of the Mass"—he would say—"since they are human works, while the Holy Mass is the work of God." [17] He was convinced that the fervour of a priest's life depended entirely upon the Mass: "The reason why a priest is lax is that he does not pay attention to the Mass! My God, how we ought to pity a priest who celebrates as if he were engaged in something routine!" [18] He was accustomed, when celebrating, also to offer his own life in sacrifice: "What a good thing it is for a priest each morning to offer himself to God in sacrifice!" [19]

This deep personal identification with the Sacrifice of the Cross led him—by a sole inward movement—from the altar to the confessional. Priests ought never to be resigned to empty confessionals or the apparent indifference of the faithful to this sacrament. In France, at the time of the Curé of Ars, confession was no more easy or frequent than in our own day, since the upheaval caused by the revolution had long inhibited the practice of religion. Yet he sought in every way, by his preaching and his powers of persuasion, to help his parishioners to rediscover the meaning and beauty of the sacrament of Penance, presenting it as an inherent demand of the Eucharistic presence. He thus created a *"virtuous" circle*. By spending long hours in church before

[16] Monnin, A., op. cit., II, pp. 430ff.
[17] Nodet, p. 105.
[18] Ibid.
[19] Ibid., p. 104.

the tabernacle, he inspired the faithful to imitate him by coming to visit Jesus with the knowledge that their parish priest would be there, ready to listen and offer forgiveness. Later, the growing numbers of penitents from all over France would keep him in the confessional for up to sixteen hours a day. It was said that Ars had become "a great hospital of souls".[20] His first biographer relates that "the grace he obtained [for the conversion of sinners] was so powerful that it would pursue them, not leaving them a moment of peace!"[21] The saintly Curé reflected something of the same idea when he said: "It is not the sinner who returns to God to beg his forgiveness, but God himself who runs after the sinner and makes him return to him."[22] "This good Saviour is so filled with love that he seeks us everywhere."[23]

We priests should feel that the following words, which he put on the lips of Christ, are meant for each of us personally: "I will charge my ministers to proclaim to sinners that I am ever ready to welcome them, that my mercy is infinite."[24] From Saint John Mary Vianney we can learn to put our unfailing trust in the sacrament of Penance, to set it once more at the centre of our pastoral concerns, and to take up the "dialogue of salvation" which it entails. The Curé of Ars dealt with different penitents in different ways. Those who came to his confessional drawn by a deep and humble longing for God's forgiveness found in him the encouragement to plunge into the "flood of divine mercy" which sweeps everything away by its vehemence. If someone was troubled by the thought of his own frailty and

[20] Monnin, A., op. cit., II, p. 293.
[21] Ibid., II, p. 10.
[22] Nodet, p. 128.
[23] Ibid., p. 50.
[24] Ibid., p. 131.

inconstancy, and fearful of sinning again, the Curé would unveil the mystery of God's love in these beautiful and touching words: "The good Lord knows everything. Even before you confess, he already knows that you will sin again, yet he still forgives you. How great is the love of our God: he even forces himself to forget the future, so that he can grant us his forgiveness!"[25] But to those who made a lukewarm and rather indifferent confession of sin, he clearly demonstrated by his own tears of pain how "abominable" this attitude was: "I weep because you don't weep",[26] he would say. "If only the Lord were not so good! But he is so good! One would have to be a brute to treat so good a Father this way!"[27] He awakened repentance in the hearts of the lukewarm by forcing them to see God's own pain at their sins reflected in the face of the priest who was their confessor. To those who, on the other hand, came to him already desirous of and suited to a deeper spiritual life, he flung open the abyss of God's love, explaining the untold beauty of living in union with him and dwelling in his presence: "Everything in God's sight, everything with God, everything to please God. . . How beautiful it is!"[28] And he taught them to pray: "My God, grant me the grace to love you as much as I possibly can."[29]

In his time the Curé of Ars was able to transform the hearts and the lives of so many people because he enabled them to experience the Lord's merciful love. Our own time urgently needs a similar proclamation and witness to the truth of Love: *Deus caritas est* (1 Jn 4:8). Thanks to the word and the

[25] Ibid., p. 130.
[26] Ibid., p. 27.
[27] Ibid., p. 139.
[28] Ibid., p. 28.
[29] Ibid., p. 77.

sacraments of Jesus, John Mary Vianney built up his flock, although he often trembled from a conviction of his personal inadequacy, and desired more than once to withdraw from the responsibilities of the parish ministry out of a sense of his unworthiness. Nonetheless, with exemplary obedience he never abandoned his post, consumed as he was by apostolic zeal for the salvation of souls. He sought to remain completely faithful to his own vocation and mission through the practice of an austere asceticism: "The great misfortune for us parish priests"—he lamented— "is that our souls grow tepid"; meaning by this that a pastor can grow dangerously inured to the state of sin or of indifference in which so many of his flock are living.[30] He himself kept a tight rein on his body, with vigils and fasts, lest it rebel against his priestly soul. Nor did he avoid self-mortification for the good of the souls in his care and as a help to expiating the many sins he heard in confession. To a priestly confrere he explained: "I will tell you my recipe: I give sinners a small penance and the rest I do in their place."[31] Aside from the actual penances which the Curé of Ars practised, the core of his teaching remains valid for each of us: souls have been won at the price of Jesus' own blood, and a priest cannot devote himself to their salvation if he refuses to share personally in the "precious cost" of redemption.

In today's world, as in the troubled times of the Curé of Ars, the lives and activity of priests need to be distinguished by *a determined witness to the Gospel*. As Pope Paul VI rightly noted, "modern man listens more willingly to witnesses than to teachers, and if he does listen to teachers, it

[30] Ibid., p. 102.
[31] Ibid., p. 189.

is because they are witnesses." [32] Lest we experience exis-
tential emptiness and the effectiveness of our ministry be
compromised, we need to ask ourselves ever anew: "Are
we truly pervaded by the word of God? Is that word truly
the nourishment we live by, even more than bread and the
things of this world? Do we really know that word? Do we
love it? Are we deeply engaged with this word to the point
that it really leaves a mark on our lives and shapes our thinking?" [33] Just as Jesus called the Twelve to be with him (cf.
Mk 3:14), and only later sent them forth to preach, so too
in our days priests are called to assimilate that "new style of
life" which was inaugurated by the Lord Jesus and taken up
by the Apostles. [34]

It was complete commitment to this "new style of life"
which marked the priestly ministry of the Curé of Ars.
Pope John XXIII, in his Encyclical Letter *Sacerdotii nostri
primordia*, published in 1959 on the first centenary of the
death of Saint John Mary Vianney, presented his asceticism with special reference to the "three evangelical counsels" which the Pope considered necessary also for diocesan
priests: "Even though priests are not bound to embrace
these evangelical counsels by virtue of the clerical state,
these counsels nonetheless offer them, as they do all the
faithful, the surest road to the desired goal of Christian
perfection." [35] The Curé of Ars lived the "evangelical counsels" in a way suited to his priestly state. His *poverty* was
not the poverty of a religious or a monk, but that proper
to a priest: while managing much money (since well-to-do

[32] *Evangelii nuntiandi*, 41.

[33] Benedict XVI, *Homily at the Chrism Mass*, 9 April 2009.

[34] Cf. Benedict XVI, *Address to the Plenary Assembly of the Congregation for
the Clergy*, 16 March 2009.

[35] P. I.

pilgrims naturally took an interest in his charitable works),
he realized that everything had been donated to his church,
his poor, his orphans, the girls of his "*Providence*",[36] his
families of modest means. Consequently, he "was rich in
giving to others and very poor for himself".[37] As he would
explain: "My secret is simple: give everything away; hold
nothing back."[38] When he lacked money, he would say
amiably to the poor who knocked at his door: "Today
I'm poor just like you, I'm one of you."[39] At the end of
his life, he could say with absolute tranquillity: "I no longer have anything. The good Lord can call me whenever
he wants!"[40] His *chastity*, too, was that demanded of a
priest for his ministry. It could be said that it was a chastity suited to one who must daily touch the Eucharist,
who contemplates it blissfully and with that same bliss offers
it to his flock. It was said of him that "he radiated chastity; the faithful would see this when he turned and gazed
at the tabernacle with loving eyes."[41] Finally, Saint John
Mary Vianney's *obedience* found full embodiment in his conscientious fidelity to the daily demands of his ministry.
We know how he was tormented by the thought of his
inadequacy for parish ministry and by a desire to flee "in
order to bewail his poor life, in solitude".[42] Only obedience and a thirst for souls convinced him to remain at his

[36] The name given to the house where more than sixty abandoned girls
were taken in and educated. To maintain this house he would do anything:
"*J'ai fait tous les commerces imaginables*", he would say with a smile (Nodet,
p. 214).

[37] Nodet, p. 216.

[38] Ibid., p. 215.

[39] Ibid., p. 216.

[40] Ibid., p. 214.

[41] Cf. ibid., p. 112.

[42] Cf. ibid., pp. 82–84; 102–3.

post. As he explained to himself and his flock: "There are no two good ways of serving God. There is only one: serve him as he desires to be served." [43] He considered this the golden rule for a life of obedience: "Do only what can be offered to the good Lord." [44]

In this context of a spirituality nourished by the practice of the evangelical counsels, I would like to invite all priests, during this Year dedicated to them, to welcome the new springtime which the Spirit is now bringing about in the Church, not least through the ecclesial movements and the new communities. "In his gifts the Spirit is multifaceted. . . . He breathes where he wills. He does so unexpectedly, in unexpected places, and in ways previously unheard of. . . but he also shows us that he works with a view to the one body and in the unity of the one body." [45] In this regard, the statement of the Decree *Presbyterorum Ordinis* continues to be timely: "While testing the spirits to discover if they be of God, priests must discover with faith, recognize with joy and foster diligently the many and varied charismatic gifts of the laity, whether these be of a humble or more exalted kind." [46] These gifts, which awaken in many people the desire for a deeper spiritual life, can benefit not only the lay faithful but the clergy as well. The communion between ordained and charismatic ministries can provide "a helpful impulse to a renewed commitment by the Church in proclaiming and bearing witness to the Gospel of hope and charity in every corner of the world".[47] I would

[43] Ibid., p. 75.
[44] Ibid., p. 76.
[45] Benedict XVI, *Homily for the Vigil of Pentecost*, 3 June 2006.
[46] No. 9.
[47] Benedict XVI, *Address to Bishop-Friends of the Focolare Movement and the Sant'Egidio Community*, 8 February 2007.

also like to add, echoing the Apostolic Exhortation *Pastores Dabo Vobis* of Pope John Paul II, that the ordained ministry has a radical "*communitarian form*" and can be exercised only in the communion of priests with their Bishop.[48] This communion between priests and their Bishop, grounded in the sacrament of Holy Orders and made manifest in Eucharistic concelebration, needs to be translated into various concrete expressions of an effective and affective priestly fraternity.[49] Only thus will priests be able to live fully the gift of celibacy and build thriving Christian communities in which the miracles which accompanied the first preaching of the Gospel can be repeated.

The Pauline Year now coming to its close invites us also to look to the Apostle of the Gentiles, who represents a splendid example of a priest entirely devoted to his ministry. "The love of Christ urges us on"—he wrote—"because we are convinced that one has died for all; therefore all have died" (2 Cor 5:14). And he adds: "He died for all, so that those who live might live no longer for themselves, but for him who died and was raised for them" (2 Cor 5:15). Could a finer programme be proposed to any priest resolved to advance along the path of Christian perfection?

Dear brother priests, the celebration of the 150th anniversary of the death of Saint John Mary Vianney (1859) follows upon the celebration of the 150th anniversary of the apparitions of Lourdes (1858). In 1959 Blessed Pope John XXIII noted that "shortly before the Curé of Ars completed his long and admirable life, the Immaculate Virgin appeared in another part of France to an innocent and

---

[48] Cf. No. 17.
[49] Cf. John Paul II, Apostolic Exhortation *Pastores Dabo Vobis*, 74.

humble girl, and entrusted to her a message of prayer and penance which continues, even a century later, to yield immense spiritual fruits. The life of this holy priest whose centenary we are commemorating in a real way anticipated the great supernatural truths taught to the seer of Massabielle. He was greatly devoted to the Immaculate Conception of the Blessed Virgin; in 1836 he had dedicated his parish church to Our Lady Conceived without Sin and he greeted the dogmatic definition of this truth in 1854 with deep faith and great joy." [50] The Curé would always remind his faithful that "after giving us all he could, Jesus Christ wishes in addition to bequeath us his most precious possession, his Blessed Mother." [51]

To the Most Holy Virgin I entrust this Year for Priests. I ask her to awaken in the heart of every priest a generous and renewed commitment to the ideal of complete self-oblation to Christ and the Church which inspired the thoughts and actions of the saintly Curé of Ars. It was his fervent prayer life and his impassioned love of Christ Crucified that enabled John Mary Vianney to grow daily in his total self-oblation to God and the Church. May his example lead all priests to offer that witness of unity with their Bishop, with one another and with the lay faithful, which today, as ever, is so necessary. Despite all the evil present in our world, the words which Christ spoke to his Apostles in the Upper Room continue to inspire us: "In the world you have tribulation; but take courage, I have overcome the world" (Jn 16:33). Our faith in the Divine Master gives us the strength to look to the future with confidence. Dear priests, Christ is counting on you. In the footsteps of the

---

[50] Encyclical Letter *Sacerdotii nostri primordia*, P. III.
[51] Nodet, p. 244.

Curé of Ars, let yourselves be enthralled by him. In this way you too will be, for the world in our time, heralds of hope, reconciliation and peace!

With my blessing.

From the Vatican, 16 June 2009.

BENEDICTVS PP. XVI

2

Letter of Pope John Paul II on the Curé of Ars

Letter of the Holy Father to All the Priests of the Church for Holy Thursday 1986

Dear Brother Priests,

Holy Thursday, the Feast of Priests

1. Here we are again, about to celebrate Holy Thursday, the day on which Christ Jesus instituted the Eucharist and at the same time our ministerial Priesthood. "Having loved his own who were in the world, he loved them to the end." [1] As the Good Shepherd, he was about to give up his life for his sheep,[2] to save man, to reconcile himself with his Father and bring him into a new life. And already at the Last Supper he offered to the Apostles as food his own Body given up for them, and his Blood shed for them.

Each year this day is an important one for all Christians: like the first disciples, they come to receive the Body and Blood of Christ in the evening liturgy that renews the Last Supper.

[1] Jn 13:1.
[2] Cf. Jn 10:11.

They receive from the Saviour his testament of fraternal love which must inspire their whole lives, and they begin to watch with him, in order to be united with him in his Passion. You yourselves gather them together and guide their prayer.

But this day is especially important for us, dear brother priests. It is the feast of priests. It is the birthday of our Priesthood, which is a sharing in the one Priesthood of Christ the Mediator. On this day the priests of the whole world are invited to concelebrate the Eucharist with their bishops and with them to renew the promises of their priestly commitment to the service of Christ and his Church.

As you know, I feel particularly close to each one of you on this occasion. And, the same as every year, as a sign of our sacramental union in the same Priesthood, and impelled by my affectionate esteem for you and by my duty to confirm all my brothers in their service of the Lord, I wish to send you this letter to help you stir up the wonderful gift that was conferred on you through the laying on of hands.[3] This ministerial Priesthood which is our lot is also our vocation and our grace. It marks our whole life with the seal of the most necessary and most demanding of services, the salvation of souls. We are led to it by a host of predecessors.

The matchless example of the Curé of Ars

2. One of those predecessors remains particularly present in the memory of the Church, and he will be especially commemorated this year, on the second centenary of his birth: Saint John Marie Vianney, the Curé of Ars. Together we wish to thank Christ, the Prince of Pastors, for this extraordinary model of priestly life and service which the saintly

[3] Cf. 2 Tim 1:6.

Curé of Ars offers to the whole Church, and above all to us priests.

How many of us prepared ourselves for the Priesthood, or today exercise the difficult task of caring for souls, having before our eyes the figure of Saint John Mary Vianney! His example cannot be forgotten. More than ever we need his witness, his intercession, in order to face the situations of our times when, in spite of a certain number of hopeful signs, evangelization is being contradicted by a growing secularization, when spiritual discipline is being neglected, when many are losing sight of the Kingdom of God, when often, even in the pastoral ministry, there is a too exclusive concern for the social aspect, for temporal aims. In the last century the Curé of Ars had to face difficulties which were perhaps of a different kind but which were no less serious. By his life and work he represented, for the society of his time, a great evangelical challenge that bore astonishing fruits of conversion. Let us not doubt that he still presents to us today that *great evangelical challenge.*

I therefore invite you now to meditate on our Priesthood in the presence of this matchless pastor who illustrates both the fullest realization of the priestly ministry and the holiness of the minister.

As you know, John Mary Baptist Vianney died at Ars on 4 August 1859, after some forty years of exhausting dedication. He was seventy-three years of age. When he arrived, Ars was a small and obscure village in the Diocese of Lyons, now in the Diocese of Belley. At the end of his life, people came from all over France, and his reputation for holiness, after he had been called home to God, soon attracted the attention of the universal Church. Saint Pius X beatified him in 1905, Pius XI canonized him in 1925, and then in 1929 declared him Patron Saint of the parish priests of the whole world. On the centenary of his death, Pope John XXIII wrote the Encyclical *Sacerdotii Nostri Primordia*, to present the Curé of Ars as a model of priestly life and asceticism, a model of pastoral zeal, and this in the context of the needs of our time. Here, I would simply like to draw your attention to certain essential points so as to help us to rediscover and live our Priesthood better.

THE TRULY EXTRAORDINARY LIFE OF THE CURÉ OF ARS

His tenacious will in preparing for the Priesthood

3. The Curé of Ars is truly a model of strong will for those preparing for the Priesthood. Many of the trials which followed one after another could have discouraged him: the effects of the upheaval of the French Revolution, the lack of opportunities for education in his rural environment, the reluctance of his father, the need for him to do his share of work in the fields, the hazards of military service. Above all, and in spite of his intuitive intelligence and lively sensitivity, there was his great difficulty in learning and memorizing, and so in following the theological courses in Latin, all of which resulted in his dismissal from the seminary in Lyons. However, after the genuineness of his vocation had finally been acknowledged, at 29 years of age he was able to be ordained. Through his tenacity in working and praying, he overcame all obstacles and limitations, just as he did later in his priestly life, by his perseverance in laboriously preparing his sermons or spending the evenings reading the works of theologians and spiritual writers. From his youth he was filled with a great desire to "win souls for the good

of God" by being a priest, and he was supported by the confidence placed in him by the parish priest of the neighboring town of Ecully, who never doubted his vocation and took charge of a good part of his training. What an example of courage for those who today experience the grace of being called to the Priesthood!

The depth of his love for Christ and for souls.

4. The Curé of Ars is a model of priestly zeal for all pastors. The secret of his generosity is to be found without doubt in *his love for God*, lived without limits, in constant response to the love made manifest *in Christ crucified*. This is where he bases his desire to do everything to save the souls ransomed by Christ at such a great price, and to bring them back to the love of God. Let us recall one of those pithy sayings which he had the knack of uttering: "The priesthood is the love of the Heart of Jesus." [4] In his sermons and catechesis he continually returned to that love: "O my God, I prefer to die loving you than to live a single instant without loving you.... I love you, my divine Saviour, because you were crucified for us ... because you have me crucified for you." [5] For the sake of Christ, he seeks to conform himself exactly to the radical demands that Jesus in the Gospels puts before the disciples whom he sends out: prayer, poverty, humility, self-denial, voluntary penance. And, like Christ, he has a love for his flock that leads him to extreme pastoral commitment and self-sacrifice. Rarely has a pastor been so acutely aware of his

[4] Cf. "Jean-Marie Vianney, curé d'Ars, sa pensée", son coeur présentés par l'Abbé Bernard Nodet, éditions Xavier Mappus, LePuy, 1958, p. 100; henceforth cited as Nodet.

[5] Nodet, p. 44.

responsibilities, so consumed by a desire to wrest his people from the sins of their lukewarmness. "O my God, grant me the conversion of my parish: I consent to suffer whatever you wish, for as long as I live."

Dear brother priests, nourished by the Second Vatican Council which has felicitously placed the priest's consecration within the framework of his pastoral mission, let us join Saint John Mary Vianney and seek the dynamism of our pastoral zeal in the Heart of Jesus, in his love for souls. If we do not draw from the same source, our ministry risks bearing little fruit!

The many wonderful fruits of his ministry

5. In the case of the Curé of Ars, the results were indeed wonderful, somewhat as with Jesus in the Gospel. Through John Mary Vianney, who consecrates his whole strength and his whole heart to him, Jesus saves souls. The Saviour entrusts them to him, in abundance.

First, *his parish*—which numbered only 230 people when he arrived—which will be profoundly changed. One recalls that in that village there was a great deal of indifference and very little religious practice among the men. The bishop had warned John Mary Vianney: "There is not much love of God in that parish, you will put some there." But quite soon, far beyond his own village, the Curé becomes *the pastor of a multitude* coming from the entire region, from different parts of France and from other countries. It is said that 80,000 came in the year 1858! People sometimes waited for days to see him, to go to confession to him. What attracted them to him was not merely curiosity nor even a reputation justified by miracles and extraordinary cures, which the saint would wish to hide. It was much more the realization of meeting a saint, amazing for his penance, so close to God in prayer, remarkable for his peace and humility in the midst of popular acclaim, and above all so intuitive in responding to the inner disposition of souls and in freeing them from their burdens, especially in the confessional. Yes, God chose as a model for pastors one who could have appeared poor, weak, defenseless and contemptible in the eyes of men.[6] He graced them with his best gifts as a guide and healer of souls.

While recognizing the special nature of the grace given to the Curé of Ars, is there not here a sign of hope for pastors today who are suffering from a kind of spiritual desert?

THE MAIN ACTS OF THE MINISTRY OF THE CURÉ OF ARS

Different apostolic approaches to what is essential

6. John Mary Vianney dedicated himself essentially to teaching the faith and to purifying consciences, and these two ministries were directed towards the Eucharist. Should we not see here, today also, the three objectives of the priest's pastoral service?

While the purpose is undoubtedly to bring the people of God together around the Eucharistic mystery by means of catechesis and penance, other apostolic approaches, varying according to circumstances, are also necessary. Sometimes it is a simple presence, over the years, with the silent witness of faith in the midst of non-Christian surroundings; or being near to people, to families and their concerns; there

---

[6] Cf. 1 Cor 1:28–29.

is a preliminary evangelization that seeks to awaken to the faith unbelievers and the lukewarm; there is the witness of charity and justice shared with Christian lay people, which makes the faith more credible and puts it into practice. These give rise to a whole series of undertakings and apostolic works which prepare or continue Christian formation. The Curé of Ars himself taxed his ingenuity to devise initiatives adapted to his time and his parishioners. However, all these priestly activities were centered on the Eucharist, catechesis and the Sacrament of Reconciliation.

The Sacrament of Reconciliation

7. It is undoubtedly his untiring devotion to the Sacrament of Reconciliation which revealed the principle charism of the Curé of Ars and is rightly the reason for his renown. It is good that such an example should encourage us today to restore to the ministry of reconciliation all the attention which it deserves and which the Synod of Bishops of 1983 so justly emphasized.[7] Without the step of conversion, penance and seeking pardon that the Church's ministers ought untiringly to encourage and welcome, the much desired renewal will remain superficial and illusory.

The first care of the Curé of Ars was to teach the faithful to desire repentance. He stressed the beauty of God's forgiveness. Was not all his priestly life and all his strength dedicated to the conversion of sinners? And it was above all in the confessional that God's mercy manifested itself. So he did not wish to get rid of the penitents who came from all parts and to whom he often devoted ten hours a day,

[7] Cf. John Paul II, Post-Synodal Apostolic Exhortation *Reconciliatio et Paenitentia* (2 December 1984): AAS 77 (1985): 185–275.

sometimes fifteen or more. For him this was undoubtedly the greatest of his mortifications, a form of martyrdom. In the first place it was a martyrdom in the physical sense from the heat, the cold or the suffocating atmosphere. Secondly in the moral sense, for he himself suffered from the sins confessed and even more the lack of repentance: "I weep because you do not weep." In the face of these indifferent people, whom he welcomed as best he could and tried to awaken in them the love of God, the Lord enabled him to reconcile great sinners who were repentant and also to guide to perfection souls thirsting for it. It was here above all that God asked him to share in the Redemption.

For our own part, we have rediscovered, better than during the last century, the community aspect of penance, preparation for forgiveness and thanksgiving after forgiveness. But sacramental forgiveness will always require a personal encounter with the crucified Christ through the mediation of his minister.[8] Unfortunately it is often the case that penitents do not fervently hasten to the confessional, as in the time of the Curé of Ars.

Now, just when a great number seem to stay away from confession completely, for various reasons, it is a sign of the urgent need to develop a whole pastoral strategy of the Sacrament of Reconciliation. This will be done by constantly reminding Christians of the need to have a real relationship with God, to have a sense of sin when one is closed to God and to others, the need to be converted and through the Church to receive forgiveness as a free gift of God. They also need to be reminded of the conditions that enable the sacrament to be celebrated well, and in this regard to overcome

[8] Cf. John Paul II, Encyclical Letter *Redemptor Hominis* (4 March 1979), no. 20: AAS 71 (1979): 313–16.

prejudices, baseless fears and routine.[9] Such a situation at the same time requires that we ourselves should remain very available for this ministry of forgiveness, ready to devote to it the necessary time and care, and I would even say giving it priority over other activities. The faithful will then realize the value that we attach to it, as did the Curé of Ars.

Of course, as I wrote in the Post-Synodal Exhortation on Penance,[10] the ministry of reconciliation undoubtedly remains the most difficult, the most delicate, the most taxing and the most demanding of all—especially when priests are in short supply. This ministry also presupposes on the part of the confessor great human qualities, above all an intense and sincere spiritual life; it is necessary that the priest himself should make regular use of this sacrament.

Always be convinced of this, dear brother priests: this ministry of mercy is one of the most beautiful and most consoling. It enables you to enlighten consciences, to forgive them and to give them fresh vigor in the name of the Lord Jesus. It enables you to be for them a spiritual physician and counsellor; it remains "the irreplaceable manifestation and the test of the priestly ministry".[11]

The Eucharist: Offering the Mass, communion, adoration

8. The two Sacraments of Reconciliation and the Eucharist remain closely linked. Without a continually renewed conversion and reception of the sacramental grace of

[9] Cf. John Paul II, Post-Synodal Apostolic Exhortation *Reconciliatio et Paenitentia* (2 December 1984): AAS 77 (1985): 250–52.

[10] Cf. ibid., no. 29: AAS 77 (1985): 252–56.

[11] John Paul II, Letter to Priests for Holy Thursday 1983, no. 3: AAS 75 (1983): pars I, p. 419.

forgiveness, participation in the Eucharist would not reach its full redemptive efficacy.[12] Just as Christ began his ministry with the words "Repent and believe in the gospel",[13] so the Curé of Ars generally began each of his days with the ministry of forgiveness. But he was happy to direct his reconciled penitents to the *Eucharist*.

The Eucharist was at the very center of his spiritual life and pastoral work. He said: "All good works put together are not equivalent to the Sacrifice of the Mass, because they are the works of men and the Holy Mass is the work of God." [14] It is in the Mass that the sacrifice of Calvary is made present for the Redemption of the world. Clearly, the priest must unite the daily gift of himself to the offering of the Mass: "How well a priest does, therefore, to offer himself to God in sacrifice every morning!" [15] "Holy Communion and the Holy Sacrifice of the Mass are the two most efficacious actions for obtaining the conversion of hearts." [16]

Thus the Mass was for John Mary Vianney the great joy and comfort of his priestly life. He took great care, despite the crowds of penitents, to spend more than a quarter of an hour in silent preparation. He celebrated with recollection, clearly expressing his adoration at the consecration and communion. He accurately remarked: "The cause of priestly laxity is not paying attention to the Mass!" [17]

The Curé of Ars was particularly mindful of the permanence of Christ's real presence in the Eucharist. It was

[12] Cf. John Paul II, Encyclical Letter *Redemptor Hominis* (4 March 1979), no. 20: AAS 71 (1979): 309–13.
[13] Mk 1:15.
[14] Nodet, p. 108.
[15] Nodet, p. 107.
[16] Nodet, p. 110.
[17] Nodet, p. 108.

generally before the tabernacle that he spent long hours in adoration, before daybreak or in the evening; it was towards the tabernacle that he often turned during his homilies, saying with emotion: "He is there!" It was also for this reason that he, so poor in his presbytery, did not hesitate to spend large sums on embellishing his Church. The appreciable result was that his parishioners quickly took up the habit of coming to pray before the Blessed Sacrament, discovering, through the attitude of their pastor, the grandeur of the mystery of faith.

With such a testimony before our eyes, we think about what the Second Vatican Council says to us today on the subject of priests: "They exercise this sacred function of Christ most of all in the Eucharistic liturgy." [18] And more recently, the Extraordinary Synod in December 1985 recalled: "The liturgy must favor and make shine brightly the sense of the sacred. It must be imbued with reverence, adoration and glorification of God.... The Eucharist is the source and summit of all the Christian life." [19]

Dear brother priests, the example of the Curé of Ars invites us to a serious examination of conscience: what place do we give the Mass in our daily lives? Is it, as on the day of our Ordination—it was our first act as priests!—the principle of our apostolic work and personal sanctification? What care do we take in preparing for it? And in celebrating it? In praying before the Blessed Sacrament? In encouraging our faithful people to do the same? In making our Churches the House of God to which the divine presence attracts the

---

[18] Second Vatican Council, Dogmatic Constitution on the Church *Lumen Gentium*, no. 28.

[19] II, B, b/1 and C/1; cf. Second Vatican Council, Dogmatic Constitution on the Church *Lumen Gentium*, no. 11.

people of our time who too often have the impression of a world empty of God?

Preaching and catechesis

9. The Curé of Ars was also careful never to neglect in any way the ministry of the Word, which is absolutely necessary in predisposing people to faith and conversion. He even said: "Our Lord, who is truth itself, considers his Word no less important than his Body." [20] We know how long he spent, especially at the beginning, in laboriously composing his Sunday sermons. Later on he came to express himself more spontaneously, always with lively and clear conviction, with images and comparisons taken from daily life and easily grasped by his flock. His catechetical instructions to the children also formed an important part of his ministry, and the adults gladly joined the children so as to profit from this matchless testimony which flowed from his heart.

He had the courage to denounce evil in all its forms; he did not keep silent, for it was a question of the eternal salvation of his faithful people: "If a pastor remains silent when he sees God insulted and souls going astray, woe to him! If he does not want to be damned, and if there is some disorder in his parish, he must trample upon human respect and the fear of being despised or hated." This responsibility was his anguish as a parish priest. But as a rule, "he preferred to show the attractive side of virtue rather than the ugliness of vice", and if he spoke—sometimes in tears— about sin and the danger for salvation, he insisted on the tenderness of God who has been offended, and the happiness

[20] Nodet, p. 126.

of being loved by God, united to God, living in his presence and for him.

Dear brother priests, you are deeply convinced of the importance of proclaiming the Gospel, which the Second Vatican Council placed in the first rank of the functions of a priest.[21] You seek, through catechesis, through preaching and in other forms which also include the media, to touch the hearts of our contemporaries, with their hopes and uncertainties, in order to awaken and foster their faith. Like the Curé of Ars and in accordance with the exhortation of the Council,[22] take care to teach the Word of God itself which calls people to conversion and holiness.

THE IDENTITY OF THE PRIEST

The specific ministry of the priest

10. Saint John Mary Vianney gives an eloquent answer to certain *questionings of the priest's identity*, which have manifested themselves in the course of the last twenty years; in fact it seems that today a more balanced position is being reached.

The priest always, and in an unchangeable way, finds the source of his identity in Christ the Priest. It is not the world which determines his status, as though it depended on changing needs or ideas about social roles. The priest is marked with the seal of the Priesthood of Christ, in order to share in his function as the one Mediator and Redeemer.

[21] Second Vatican Council, Decree on the Ministry and Life of Priests *Presbyterorum Ordinis*, no. 3.
[22] Cf. ibid.

So, because of this fundamental bond, there opens before the priest the immense field of the service of souls, for their salvation in Christ and in the Church. This service must be completely inspired by love of souls in imitation of Christ who gives his life for them. It is God's wish that all people should be saved, and that none of the little ones should be lost.[23] "The priest must always be ready to respond to the needs of souls", said the Curé of Ars.[24] "He is not for himself, he is for you."[25]

The priest is for the laity: he animates them and supports them in the exercise of the common priesthood of the baptized—so well illustrated by the Second Vatican Council—which consists in their making their lives a spiritual offering, in witnessing to the Christian spirit in the family, in taking charge of the temporal sphere and sharing in the evangelization of their brethren. But the service of the priest belongs to another order. He is ordained to act in the name of Christ the Head, to bring people into the new life made accessible by Christ, to dispense to them the mysteries—the Word, forgiveness, the Bread of Life—to gather them into his body, to help them to form themselves from within, to live and to act according to the saving plan of God. In a word, our identity as priests is manifested in the "creative" exercise of the love for souls communicated by Christ Jesus.

Attempts to make the priest more like the laity are damaging to the Church.

This does not mean in any way that the priest can remain remote from the human concerns of the laity: he must be very near to them, as John Mary Vianney was, but as a

[23] Cf. Mt 18:14.
[24] Nodet, p. 101.
[25] Nodet, p. 102.

priest, always in a perspective which is that of their salvation and of the progress of the Kingdom of God. He is the
witness and the dispenser of a life other than earthly life.[26]
It is essential to the Church that the identity of the priest
be safeguarded, with its vertical dimension. The life and
personality of the Curé of Ars are a particularly enlighten-
ing and vigorous illustration of this.

His intimate configuration to Christ and his solidarity with sinners

11. Saint John Marie Vianney did not content himself with
the ritual carrying out of the activities of his ministry. It
was his heart and his life which he sought to conform to
Christ.

Prayer was the soul of his life: silent and contemplative prayer,
generally in his church at the foot of the tabernacle. Through
Christ, his soul opened to the three divine Persons, to whom
he would entrust "his poor soul" in his last will and testament. "He kept a constant union with God in the middle of
an extremely busy life." And he did not neglect the office or
the rosary. He turned spontaneously to the Virgin.

His *poverty* was extraordinary. He literally stripped himself of everything for the poor. And he shunned honors.
Chastity shone in his face. He knew the value of purity in
order "to rediscover the source of love which is God." *Obedience* to Christ consisted, for John Mary Vianney, in obedience to the Church and especially to the Bishop. This
obedience took the form of accepting the heavy charge of
being a parish priest, which often frightened him.

[26] Cf. Second Vatican Council, Decree on the Ministry and Life of Priests
Presbyterorum Ordinis, no. 3.

But the Gospel insists especially on *renouncing self,* on accepting the Cross. Many were the crosses which presented themselves to the Curé of Ars in the course of his ministry: calumny on the part of the people, being misunderstood by an assistant priest or other confreres, contradictions, and also a mysterious struggle against the powers of hell, and sometimes even the temptation to despair in the midst of spiritual darkness.

Nonetheless he did not content himself with just accepting these trials without complaining; he went beyond them by *mortification,* imposing on himself continual fasts and many other rugged practices in order to "reduce his body to servitude", as Saint Paul says. But what we must see clearly in this penance, which our age unhappily has little taste for, are his motives: love of God and the conversion of sinners. Thus he asks a discouraged fellow priest: "You have prayed . . . , you have wept . . . , but have you fasted, have you kept vigil . . . ?" [27] Here we are close to the warning Jesus gave to the Apostles: "But this kind is cast out only by prayer and fasting." [28]

In a word, John Mary Vianney sanctified himself so as to be more able to sanctify others. Of course, conversion remains the secret of hearts, which are free in their actions, and the secret of God's grace. By his ministry, the priest can only enlighten people, guide them in the internal forum and give them the sacraments. The sacraments are of course actions of Christ, and their effectiveness is not diminished by the imperfection or unworthiness of the minister. But the results depend also on the dispositions of those who receive them, and these are greatly assisted by the personal holiness of the

[27] Nodet, p. 193.
[28] Mt 17:21.

priest, by his perceptible witness, as also by the mysterious exchange of merits in the Communion of Saints. Saint Paul said: "In my flesh I complete what is lacking in Christ's afflictions for the sake of his body, that is, the Church." [29] John Mary Vianney in a sense wished to force God to grant these graces of conversion, not only by his prayer but by the sacrifice of his whole life. He wished to love God for those who did not love him, and even to do the penance which they would not do. He was truly a pastor completely at one with his sinful people.

Dear brother priests, let us not be afraid of this very personal commitment—marked by asceticism and inspired by love—which God asks of us for the proper exercise of our Priesthood. Let us remember the recent reflections of the Synodal Fathers: "It seems to us that in the difficulties of today God wishes to teach us more deeply the value, importance and central place of the Cross of Jesus Christ." [30] In the priest, Christ relives his Passion, for the sake of souls. Let us give thanks to God who thus permits us to share in the Redemption, in our hearts and in our flesh!

For all these reasons, Saint John Mary Vianney never ceases to be a witness, ever living, ever relevant, to the truth about the priestly vocation and service. We recall the convincing way in which he spoke of the greatness of the priest and of the absolute need for him. Those who are already priests, those who are preparing for the Priesthood and those who will be called to it must fix their eyes on his example and follow it. The faithful too will more clearly grasp, thanks to him, the mystery of the Priesthood of their priests. No, *the figure of the Curé of Ars does not fade.*

---

[29] Col 1:24.
[30] Final Report, D/2.

Conclusion: For Holy Thursday

12. Dear Brothers, may these reflections renew your joy at being priests, your desire to be priests more profoundly! The witness of the Curé of Ars contains still other treasures to be discovered. We shall return to these themes at greater length during the pilgrimage which I shall have the joy of making next October, since the French Bishops have invited me to Ars in honor of the second centenary of the birth of John Mary Vianney.

I address this first meditation to you, dear brothers, for the Solemnity of Holy Thursday. In each of our diocesan communities we are going to gather together, on this birthday of our Priesthood, to renew the grace of the Sacrament of Orders, to stir up the love which is the mark of our vocation.

We hear Christ saying to us as he said to the Apostles: "Greater love has no man than this, that a man lay down his life for his friends. . . . No longer do I call you servants . . . , I have called you friends." [31]

Before him who manifests love in its fullness, we, priests and Bishops, renew our priestly commitments.

We pray for one another, each for his brother, and all for all.

We ask the eternal Father that the memory of the Curé of Ars may help to stir up our zeal in his service.

We beseech the Holy Spirit to call to the Church's service many priests of the calibre and holiness of the Curé of Ars: in our age she has so great a need of them, and she is no less capable of bringing such vocations to full flower.

And we entrust our Priesthood to the Virgin Mary, the Mother of priests, to whom John Mary Vianney ceaselessly

[31] Jn 15:13–15.

had recourse with tender affection and total confidence. This was for him another reason for giving thanks: "Jesus Christ," he said, "having given us all that he could give us, also wishes to make us heirs of what is most precious to him, his holy Mother." [32]

For my part, I assure you once more of my great affection, and, with your Bishop, I send to you my Apostolic Blessing.

From the Vatican, 16 March 1986, the Fifth Sunday of Lent, in the eighth year of my Pontificate.

[32] Nodet, p. 252.

3

Encyclical of Pope John XXIII
on St. John Vianney
Sacerdotii Nostri Primordia

To Our Venerable Brethren, the Patriarchs, Primates, Archbishops, Bishops, and other Local Ordinaries in Peace and Communion with the Apostolic See.

Venerable Brethren, Health and Apostolic Benediction.

When We think of the first days of Our priesthood, which were so full of joyous consolations, We are reminded of one event that moved Us to the very depths of Our soul: the sacred ceremonies that were carried out so majestically in the Basilica of St. Peter's on January 8, 1905, when John Mary Baptist Vianney, a very humble French priest, was enrolled in the lists of the Blessed in Heaven. Our own ordination to the priesthood had taken place a few short months before, and it filled Us with wonder to see the delight of Our predecessor of happy memory, St. Pius X (who had once been the parish priest of the town of Salzano), as he offered this wonderful model of priestly virtues to all those entrusted with the care of souls, for their imitation. Now as We look back over the span of so many years, We never

Latin Text: *Acta Apostolicae Sedis*, 51 (1959): 545–79; English Translation: *The Pope Speaks*, 6 (Winter, 1959/60), 7–33.

stop giving thanks to Our Redeemer for this wonderful
blessing, which marked the beginning of Our priestly ministry and served as an effective heavenly incentive to virtue.

2. It is all the easier to remember, because on the very same
day on which the honors of the Blessed were attributed to
this holy man, word reached Us of the elevation of that wonderful prelate, Giacomo M. Radini-Tedeschi, to the dignity
of Bishop; a few days later, he was to call Us to assist him in
his work, and We found him a most loving teacher and guide.
It was in his company that, early in 1905, We made Our first
pious pilgrimage to the tiny village called Ars, that had become
so famous because of the holiness of its Curé.

3. Again, We cannot help thinking that it was through a
special design of God's providence that the year in which We
became a Bishop—1925—was the very one in which, toward
the end of May, the Supreme Pontiff of happy memory, Pius
XI, accorded the honors of sainthood to the humble Curé
of Ars. In his talk on that occasion, the Supreme Pontiff chose
to remind everyone of "the gaunt figure of John Baptist Vianney, with that head shining with long hair that resembled a
snowy crown, and that thin face, wasted from long fasting,
where the innocence and holiness of the meekest and humblest of souls shone forth so clearly that the first sight of it
called crowds of people back to thoughts of salvation".[1] A short
while after, this same predecessor of Ours took the occasion
of the 50th anniversary of his own ordination to the priesthood to designate St. John Mary Vianney (to whose patron-
age St. Pius X had previously committed all of the shepherds
of souls in France) as the heavenly patron of all "pastors, to
promote their spiritual welfare throughout the world".[2]

[1] AAS 17 (1925): 224.
[2] Apostolic letter *Anno iubilari*, AAS 21 (1929): 313.

A Time for Tribute

4. We have thought it opportune to use an Encyclical Letter to recall these acts of Our Predecessors that are so closely bound up with such happy memories, Venerable Brethren, now that We are approaching the 100th anniversary of the day—August 4, 1859—on which this holy man, completely broken from forty years of the most tireless and exhausting labors, and already famous in every corner of the world for his holiness, passed on most piously to his heavenly reward.

5. And so We give thanks to God in His goodness, not only for seeing to it that this Saint would twice cast the brilliant light of his holiness over Our priestly life at moments of great importance, but also for offering Us an opportunity here at the beginning of Our Pontificate to pay solemn tribute to this wonderful shepherd of souls on this happy 100th anniversary. It will be easy for you to see, Venerable Brethren, that We are directing this letter principally to Our very dearest sons, those in sacred orders, and urging each and every one of them—especially those engaged in pastoral ministry—to devote all their attention to a consideration of the wonderful example of this holy man, who once shared in this priestly work and who now serves as their heavenly patron.

Earlier Popes on the Priesthood

6. The Supreme Pontiffs have issued many documents reminding those in sacred orders of the greatness of their priestly office, and pointing out the safest and surest way for them to carry out their duties properly. To recall only the more recent and more important of these, We would like to make special mention of the Apostolic Exhortation

of St. Pius X of happy memory entitled *"Haerent Animo"*,[3] issued early in Our priesthood, which urged Us on to greater efforts to achieve a more ardent devotion, and the wonderful encyclical of our predecessor of happy memory, Pius XI, that began with the words *"Ad catholici sacerdotii"*,[4] and finally the Apostolic Exhortation *"Menti Nostrae"* [5] of Our immediate predecessor, along with his three allocutions on the occasion of the canonization of St. Pius X that give so clear and complete a picture of sacred orders.[6] Undoubtedly you are familiar with all of these documents, Venerable Brethren. But permit Us also to mention a few words from a sermon published after the death of Our immediate predecessor; they stand as the final solemn exhortation of that great Pontiff to priestly holiness: "Through the character of Sacred Orders, God willed to ratify that eternal covenant of love, by which He loves His priests above all others; and they are obliged to repay God for this special love with holiness of life. . . . So a cleric should be considered as a man chosen and set apart from the midst of the people, and blessed in a very special way with heavenly gifts—a sharer in divine power, and, to put it briefly, another Christ. . . . He is no longer supposed to live for himself; nor can he devote himself to the interests of just his own relatives, or friends or native land. . . . He must be aflame with charity toward everyone. Not even his thoughts, his will, his feelings belong to him, for they are rather those of Jesus Christ who is his life." [7]

[3] *Acta Pii* X, IV, pp. 237–64.

[4] AAS 28 (1936) 5–53.

[5] AAS 42 (1950) 657–702.

[6] AAS 46 (1954) 313–17, 666–77; TPS v. l, no. 2, pp. 147–58.

[7] Cf. AAS 50 (1958) 966–67.

Subject of the Encyclical

7. St. John Mary Vianney is a person who attracts and practically pushes all of us to these heights of the priestly life. And so We are pleased to add Our own exhortations to the others, in the hope that the priests of Our day may exert every possible effort in this direction. We are well aware of their devoted care and interest, and well acquainted with the difficulties they face each day in their apostolic activity. And even though We regret the fact that the surging currents of this world overwhelm the spirit and courage of some and make them grow tired and inactive, We also know from experience how many more stand firm in their faith despite many hardships, and how many constantly strive to stir up an ardent zeal for the very highest ideals in their own souls. And yet, when they became priests, Christ the Lord spoke these words so full of consolation to all of them: "I no longer call you servants but friends." [8] May this encyclical of Ours help the whole clergy to foster this divine friendship and grow in it, for it is the main source of the joy and the fruitfulness of any priestly work.

8. We have no intention, Venerable Brethren, of taking up each and every matter that has any reference to the life of a priest in the present day; as a matter of fact, following closely in the footsteps of St. Pius X, "We will not say anything that you have not already heard before, nor anything that will be completely new to anyone, but rather We will concentrate on recalling things that everyone ought to remember." [9] For a mere sketch of the qualities of this Heavenly soul, if done properly, is enough to lead us readily to a serious consideration of certain things that are, it is

[8] *Pontificale Rom.*; cf. John 15:15.
[9] Exhortation *Haerent animo, Acta Pii X*, IV, p. 238.

true, necessary in every age, but which now seem to be so important that Our Apostolic office and duty force Us to put special emphasis on them on the occasion of this centenary.

A Model for the Clergy

9. The Catholic Church, which elevated this man in sacred orders, who was "wonderful in his pastoral zeal, in his devotion to prayer and in the ardor of his penance"[10] to the honors of the saints of heaven, now, one hundred years after his death, offers him with maternal joy to all the clergy as an outstanding model of priestly asceticism, of piety, especially in the form of devotion to the Eucharist, and, finally, of pastoral zeal.

I

10. You cannot begin to speak of St. John Mary Vianney without automatically calling to mind the picture of a priest who was outstanding in a unique way in voluntary affliction of his body; his only motives were the love of God and the desire for the salvation of the souls of his neighbors, and this led him to abstain almost completely from food and from sleep, to carry out the harshest kinds of penances, and to deny himself with great strength of soul. Of course, not all of the faithful are expected to adopt this kind of life; and yet divine providence has seen to it that there has never been a time when the Church did not have some pastors of souls of this kind who, under the inspiration of the Holy Spirit, did not hesitate for a moment to

[10] Prayer of the Mass on the feast of St. John Mary Vianney.

enter on this path, most of all because this way of life is particularly successful in bringing many men who have been drawn away by the allurement of error and vice back to the path of good living.

The Evangelical Counsels

11. The wonderful devotion in this regard of St. John Vianney—a man who was "hard on himself, and gentle with others" [11]—was so outstanding that it should serve as a clear and timely reminder of the important role that priests should attribute to the virtue of penance in striving for perfection in their own lives. Our predecessor of happy memory, Pius XII, in order to give a clear picture of this doctrine and to clear up the doubts and errors that bothered some people, denied that "the clerical state—as such, and on the basis of divine law—requires, of its very nature or at least as a result of some demand arising from its nature, that those enrolled in it observe the evangelical counsels", [12] and justly concluded with these words: "Hence a cleric is not bound by virtue of divine law to the evangelical counsels of poverty, chastity, obedience." [13]

12. And yet it would undoubtedly be both a distortion of the real mind of this same Supreme Pontiff (who was so interested in the sanctity of the clergy) and a contradiction of the perpetual teaching of the Church in this matter, if anyone should dare to infer from this that clerics were any less bound by their office than religious to strive for evangelical perfection of life. The truth is just

[11] Cf. *Archiv. Secr. Vat.*, C.SS. Rituum, *Processus*, v. 227, p. 196.
[12] Allocution *Annus sacer*, AAS 43 (1951): 29.
[13] Ibid.

the opposite; for the proper exercise of the priestly functions "requires a greater interior holiness than is demanded by the religious state".[14] And even if churchmen are not commanded to embrace these evangelical counsels by virtue of their clerical state, it still remains true that in their efforts to achieve holiness, these counsels offer them and all of the faithful the surest road to the desired goal of Christian perfection. What a great consolation it is to Us to realize that at the present time many generous hearted priests are showing that they realize this; even though they belong to the diocesan clergy, they have sought the help and aid of certain pious societies approved by Church authorities in order to find a quicker and easier way to move along the road to perfection.

13. Fully convinced as they are that the "highest dignity of the priesthood consists in the imitation of Christ"[15], churchmen must pay special attention to this warning of their Divine Master: "If anyone wishes to come after me, let him deny himself, and take up his cross and follow me."[16] It is recorded that "the holy parish priest of Ars often thought these words of the Lord over carefully, and determined to apply them to his own actions."[17] He made the resolution readily, and with the help of God's grace and by constant effort, he kept it to a wonderful extent; his example in the various works of priestly asceticism still points out the safest path to follow, and in the midst of this example, his poverty, chastity and obedience stand forth in a brilliant light.

---

[14] St. Thomas, *Summa Theologiae* II–II, q. 184, a. 8, in c.
[15] Cf. Pius XII, Allocution, 16 April 1953: AAS 45 (1953): 288.
[16] Matt 16:24.
[17] Cf. *Archiv. Secret. Vat.*, v. 227, p. 42.

Above: The pulpit from which St. John Vianney preached at St. Sixtus Parish in Ars. *Photograph by Mark Cusick.*

Right: The catechetical desk where the Curé spent many hours instructing the children of the parish. *Photograph by Fr. Benjamin Bradshaw(?)*

Above: The simple residence of the Curé of Ars. *Photograph by Fr. Carter Griffin.*

Opposite, top: The bedroom of St. John Vianney as it appeared during his lifetime. *Photograph by Neil J. Pfeifer.*

Opposite, bottom: The Curé's kitchen, where he would often receive guests. The pot on the hearth is where he would prepare his simple meals, often just a boiled potato. *Photograph by Mark Cusick.*

Above: The Curé's favorite statue of the Virgin Mary, in the Lady Altar of his parish. *Photograph by Fr. Benj min Sawyer.*

bove: The confessional, where countless hours were spent by the saint hearing the confessions not only of parishioners, but of penitents who traveled from miles around. *Photograph by Fr. Carter Griffin.*

The orphanage, Providence. For many years the Curé would have his lunch here with the orphan children. *Photograph by Mark Cusick.*

Opposite: The altar in the Basilica at Ars contains a reliquary holding the incorrupt body of St. John Vianney. *Photographs by Fr. Benjamin Sawyer.*

Above: The Curé's vestments. *Photograph by Ben Pohl.*

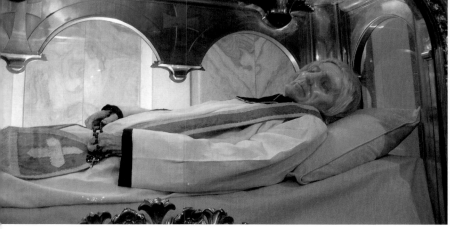

The nearby town of Paray-le-Monial, where St. Margaret Mary Alacoque received visions of the Sacred Heart. *Photograph by Adrian Tan Chong Beng.*

JE TE CONSTITUE HERITIERE DE MON CŒUR

A statue of St. Margaret Mary Alacoque at Paray-le-Monial. *Photograph by Mark Cusick.*

The Poverty of St. John Vianney

14. First of all, you have clear testimony of his poverty. The humble Curé of Ars was careful to imitate the Patriarch of Assisi in this regard, for he had accepted his rule in the Third Order of St. Francis and he carefully observed it.[18] He was rich in his generosity toward others but the poorest of men in dealing with himself; he passed a life that was almost completely detached from the changeable, perishable goods of this world, and his spirit was free and unencumbered by impediments of this kind, so that it could always lie open to those who suffered from any kind of misery; and they flocked from everywhere to seek his consolation. "My secret"—he said—"is easy to learn. It can be summed up in these few words: give everything away and keep nothing for yourself."[19]

15. This detachment from external goods enabled him to offer the most devoted and touching care to the poor, especially those in his own parish. He was very kind and gentle toward them and embraced them "with a sincere love, with the greatest of kindness, indeed with reverence".[20] He warned that the needy were never to be spurned since a disregard for them would reach in turn to God. When beggars knocked at his door, he received them with love and was very happy to be able to say to them: "I am living in need myself; I am one of you."[21] And toward the end of his life, he used to enjoy saying things like this: "I will be happy when I go; for now I no longer have any possessions; and so when God in his

[18] Cf. ibid., v. 227, p. 13i.
[19] Cf. ibid., v. 227, p. 92.
[20] Cf. ibid., v. 3897, p. 510.
[21] Cf. ibid., v. 227 p. 334.

goodness sees fit to call me, I will be ready and willing to go." [22]

16. All of this will give you a clear idea of what We have in mind, Venerable Brethren, when We exhort all of Our beloved sons who share in the priesthood to give careful thought to this example of poverty and charity. "Daily experience shows"—wrote Pius XI, with St. John Mary Vianney specifically in mind—"that priests who live modestly and follow the teaching of the Gospel by paying little attention to their own interests, always confer wonderful benefits on the Christian people".[23] And the same Supreme Pontiff issued this serious warning to priests as well as to others in the course of a discussion of the current problems of society: "When they look around and see men ready to sell anything for money and to strike a bargain for anything at all, let them pass right through the midst of these attractions of vice without a thought or care for their own desires; and let them in their holiness spurn this base pursuit of wealth, and look for the riches of souls rather than for money, and let them long for and seek God's glory rather than their own." [24]

The Use of Possessions

17. It is very important for these words to sink deep into the mind of every priest. If someone owns things that are rightfully his, let him be careful not to hang on to them greedily. Instead he should remember that the prescriptions of the Code of Canon Law dealing with church benefices make it clear that he has a serious obligation "to use

---

[22] Cf. ibid., v. 227 p. 305.

[23] Encyclical letter *Divini Redemptoris*, AAS 29 (1937): 99.

[24] Encyclical letter *Ad catholici sacerdotii*, AAS 28 (1936): 28.

superfluous income for the poor or for pious causes".[25] May
God grant that no one of Us ever lets that terrible sentence
that the parish priest of Ars once used in rebuking his flock
fall on him: "There are many people keeping their money
hidden away while many others are dying of hunger."[26]

18. We know very well that at the present time there are
many priests living in great need themselves. When they
stop to realize that heavenly honors have been paid to one
of their own who voluntarily gave up all he had and asked
for nothing more than to be the poorest of all in his parish,[27] they have a wonderful source of inspiration for devoting themselves carefully and constantly to fostering evangelical
poverty. And if Our paternal interest can offer any consolation, We want them to know that We are very happy that
they are serving Christ and the Church so generously with
no thought of their own interests.

Unbecoming Indigence

19. However, even though We praise and extol this wonderful virtue of poverty so much, no one should conclude
that We have any intention of giving Our approval to the
unbecoming indigence and misery in which the ministers
of the Lord are sometimes forced to live, both in cities and
in remote rural areas. In this regard, when St. Bede the
Venerable explained and commented on the words of the
Lord on detachment from earthly things, he excluded possible incorrect interpretations of this passage with these words:
"You must not think that this command was given with
the intention of having the saints keep no money at all for

[25] C.I.C., can. 1473.
[26] Cf. Sermons du B. Jean B.M. Vianney, 1909, v. 1, p. 364.
[27] Cf. Archiv. Secret. Vat., v. 227, p. 91.

their own use or for that of the poor (for we read that the Lord himself ... had money-boxes in forming his Church ...) but rather the idea was that this should not be the motive for serving God nor should justice be abandoned out of fear of suffering want."[28] Besides, the laborer is worthy of his hire,[29] and We share the feelings of Our immediate predecessor in urging the faithful to respond quickly and generously to the appeals of their pastors; We also join him in praising these shepherds for their efforts to see to it that those who help them in the sacred ministry do not lack the necessities of life.[30]

Model of Chastity

20. John M. Vianney was an outstanding model of voluntary mortification of the body as well as of detachment from external things. "There is only one way"—he used to say— "for anyone to devote himself to God as he should through self-denial and the practice of penance: that is by devoting himself to it completely."[31] Throughout his whole life, the holy Curé of Ars carried this principle into practice energetically in the matter of chastity.

21. This wonderful example of chastity seems to have special application to the priests of our time who—as is unfortunately the case in many regions—are often forced by the office they have assumed to live in the midst of a human society that is infected by a general looseness in morals and a spirit of unbridled lust. How often this phrase of St. Thomas Aquinas is proved true: "It is harder to lead a

[28] *In Lucae Evangelium Expositio*, IV, in c. 12; Migne, PL 92, col. 494–95.
[29] Cf. Luke 10:7.
[30] Cf. apostolic exhortation *Menti Nostrae*, AAS 42 (1950): 697–99.
[31] Cf. *Archiv. Secret. Vat.*, v. 227, p. 91.

good life in the work of caring for souls, because of the external dangers involved"[32] To this We might add the fact that they often feel themselves cut off from the society of others and that even the faithful to whose salvation they are dedicated do not understand them and offer them little help or support in their undertakings.

22. We want to use this letter, Venerable Brethren, to exhort, again and again, all of them, and especially those who are working alone and in the midst of very serious dangers of this kind, to let their whole life, so to say, resound with the splendor of holy chastity; St. Pius X had good reason to call this virtue the "choicest adornment of our order".[33]

23. Venerable Brethren, do all you can and spare no effort to see to it that the clergy entrusted to your care may enjoy living and working conditions that will best foster and be of service to their ardent zeal. This means that every effort should be exerted to eliminate the dangers that arise from too great an isolation, to issue timely warnings against unwise or imprudent actions, and last of all to check the dangers of idleness or of too much external activity. In this regard, you should recall the wise directives issued by Our immediate Predecessor in the Encyclical *Sacra Virginitas*.[34]

St. John Vianney on Chastity

24. It is said that the face of the Pastor of Ars shone with an angelic purity.[35] And even now anyone who turns toward him in mind and spirit cannot help being struck, not merely

[32] *Summa Theologiae* II-II, q. 184, a. 8, in c.
[33] Exhortation *Haerent animo; Acta Pii* X, IV, p. 260.
[34] AAS 46 (1954): 161–91; TPS (1954) v. 1, no. 1, pp. 101–23.
[35] Cf. *Archiv. Secret. Vat.*, v. 3897, p. 536.

by the great strength of soul with which this athlete of Christ reduced his body to slavery,[36] but also by the great persuasive powers he exercised over the pious crowds of pilgrims who came to him and were drawn by his heavenly meekness to follow in his footsteps. From his daily experiences in the Sacrament of Penance he got an unmistakable picture of the terrible havoc that is wrought by impure desire. This was what brought cries like these bursting from his breast: "If there were not very innocent souls to please God and make up for our offenses, how many terrible punishments we would have to suffer!" His own observations in this regard led him to offer this encouragement and advice to his hearers: "The works of penance abound in such delights and joys that once they have been tasted, nothing will ever again root them out of the soul.... Only the first steps are difficult for those who eagerly choose this path."[37]

Priest's Chastity as Help to Others

25. The ascetic way of life, by which priestly chastity is preserved, does not enclose the priest's soul within the sterile confines of his own interests, but rather it makes him more eager and ready to relieve the needs of his brethren. St. John Mary Vianney has this pertinent comment to make in this regard: "A soul adorned with the virtue of chastity cannot help loving others; for it has discovered the source and font of love—God." What great benefits are conferred on human society by men like this who are free of the cares of the world and totally dedicated to the divine ministry so that they can employ their lives, thoughts, powers

---

[36] Cf. 1 Cor 9:27.
[37] Cf. *Archiv. Secret. Vat.*, v. 3897, p. 304.

in the interest of their brethren! How valuable to the Church are priests who are anxious to preserve perfect chastity! For We agree with Our predecessor of happy memory, Pius XI, in regarding this as the outstanding adornment of the Catholic priesthood and as something "that seems to Us to correspond better to the counsels and wishes of the Most Sacred Heart of Jesus, so far as the souls of priests are concerned".[38] Was not the mind of John Mary Vianney soaring to reach the counsels of this same divine charity when he wrote this lofty sentence: "Is the priesthood love of the Most Sacred Heart of Jesus?" [39]

The Obedience of St. John Vianney

27. There are many pieces of evidence of how this man was also outstanding in the virtue of obedience. It would be true to say that the fidelity toward his superiors in the Church which he pledged at the time he became a priest and which he preserved unshaken throughout his life drove him to an uninterrupted immolation of his will for forty years.

28. All his life he longed to lead a quiet and retired life in the background, and he regarded pastoral duties as a very heavy burden laid on his shoulders and more than once he tried to free himself of it. His obedience to his bishop was admirable; We would like to mention a few instances of it in this encyclical, Venerable Brethren: "From the age of fifteen on, he ardently desired a solitary life, and as long as this wish was not fulfilled, he felt cut off from every advantage and every consolation that his state of life might have offered":[40] but "God never allowed this aim to be achieved.

[38] Encyclical letter *Ad catholici sacerdotii*, AAS 28 (1936): 28.
[39] Cf. *Archiv. Secret Vat.*, v. 227, p. 29.
[40] Cf. ibid., c. 227, p. 74.

Undoubtedly, this was God's way of bending St. John Mary Vianney's will to obedience and of teaching him to put the duties of his office before his own desires; and so there was never a time when his devotion to self-denial did not shine forth";[41] "out of complete obedience to his superiors, John M. Vianney carried out his tasks as pastor of Ars, and remained in that office till the end of his mortal life."[42]

29. It should be noted, however, that this full obedience of his to the commands of his superiors rested on supernatural principles; in acknowledging and duly obeying ecclesiastical authority, he was paying the homage of faith to the words of Christ the Lord as He told His Apostles "He who hears you, hears me."[43] To conform himself faithfully to the will of his superiors he habitually restrained his own will, whether in accepting the holy burdens of hearing Confessions, or in performing zealously for his colleagues in the apostolate such work as would produce richer and more saving fruits.

The Importance of Obedience

30. We are offering clerics this total obedience as a model, with full confidence that its force and beauty will lead them to strive for it more ardently. And if there should be someone who dares to cast doubt on the supreme importance of this virtue—as sometimes happens at the present time—let him take to heart these words of Our predecessor of happy memory, Pius XII, which everyone should keep firmly in mind: "The holiness of any life and the effectiveness of any

[41] Cf. ibid., v. 227, p. 39.
[42] Cf. ibid., v. 3895, p. 153.
[43] Luke 10:16.

apostolate has constant and faithful obedience to the hier-
archy as its solid foundation, basis and support." [44]

31. For, as you well know, Venerable Brethren, Our most
recent predecessors have often issued serious warnings to
priests about the extent of the dangers that are arising among
the clergy from a growing carelessness about obedience with
regard to the teaching authority of the Church, to the various ways and means of undertaking the apostolate, and to
ecclesiastical discipline.

An Exhortation to Obedience

32. We do not want to spend a lot of time on this, but We
think it timely to exhort all of Our sons who share in the
Catholic priesthood to foster a love in their souls that will
make them feel attached to Mother Church by ever closer
bonds, and then to make that love grow.

33. It is said that St. John M. Vianney lived in the Church
in such a way that he worked for it alone, and burned himself up like a piece of straw being consumed on fiery coals.
May that flame which comes from the Holy Spirit reach
those of Us who have been raised to the priesthood of Jesus
Christ and consume us too.

34. We owe ourselves and all we have to the Church;
may we work each day only in her name and by her authority and may we properly carry out the duties committed to
us, and may we be joined together in fraternal unity and
thus strive to serve her in that perfect way in which she
ought to be served. [45]

---

[44] Exhortation *In auspicando*, AAS 40 (1948): 375.
[45] Cf. *Archiv. Secret. Vat.*, v 227, p. 136.

II

35. St. John M. Vianney, who, as We have said, was so devoted to the virtue of penance, was just as sure that "a priest must be specially devoted to constant prayer." [46] In this regard, We know that shortly after he was made pastor of a village where Christian life had been languishing for a long time, he began to spend long and happy hours at night (when he might have been resting) in adoration of Jesus in the Sacrament of His love. The Sacred Tabernacle seemed to be the spring from which he constantly drew the power that nourished his own piety and gave new life to it and promoted the effectiveness of his apostolic labor to such an extent that the wonderful words that Our predecessor of happy memory, Pius XII, used to describe the ideal Christian parish, might well have been applied to the town of Ars in the time of this holy man: "In the middle stands the temple; in the middle of the temple the Sacred Tabernacle, and on either side the confessionals where supernatural life and health are restored to the Christian people." [47]

Prayer in the Life of St. John Vianney

36. How timely and how profitable this example of constant prayer on the part of a man completely dedicated to caring for the needs of souls is for priests in Our own day, who are likely to attribute too much to the effectiveness of external activity and stand ready and eager to immerse themselves in the hustle and bustle of the ministry, to their own spiritual detriment!

[46] Cf. ibid., v. 227, p. 33.
[47] Cf. *Discorsi e radiomessaggi* di S.S. Pio XII, v. 14, p. 452.

37. "The thing that keeps us priests from gaining sanctity"—
the Cure of Ars used to say—"is thoughtlessness. It annoys
us to turn our minds away from external affairs; we don't know
what we really ought to do. What we need is deep reflection, together with prayer and an intimate union with God."
The testimony of his life makes it clear that he always remained
devoted to his prayers and that not even the duty of hearing
confessions or any other pastoral office could cause him to
neglect them. "Even in the midst of tremendous labors, he
never let up on his conversation with God." [48]

38. But listen to his own words; for he seemed to have
an inexhaustible supply of them whenever he talked about
the happiness or the advantages that he found in prayer:
"We are beggars who must ask God for everything";[49] "How
many people we can call back to God by our prayers!" [50]
And he used to say over and over again: "Ardent prayer
addressed to God: this is man's greatest happiness on earth!" [51]

39. And he enjoyed this happiness abundantly when his
mind rose with the help of heavenly light to contemplate
the things of heaven and his pure and simple soul rose with
all its deepest love from the mystery of the Incarnation to
the heights of the Most Holy Trinity. And the crowds of
pilgrims who surrounded him in the temple could feel something coming forth from the depths of the inner life of this
humble priest when words like these burst forth from his
inflamed breast, as they often did: "To be loved by God, to
be joined to God, to walk before God, to live for God: O
blessed life, O blessed death!" [52]

[48] Cf. *Archiv. Secret. Vat.*, v. 227, p. 131.
[49] Cf. ibid., v. 227, p. 1100.
[50] Cf. ibid., v. 227, p. 54.
[51] Cf. ibid., v. 227, p. 45.
[52] Cf. ibid., v. 227, p. 29.

Necessity of Prayer Life

40. We sincerely hope, Venerable Brethren, that these lessons from the life of St. John M. Vianney may make all of the sacred ministers committed to your care feel sure that they must exert every effort to be outstanding in their devotion to prayer; this can really be done, even if they are very busy with apostolic labors.

41. But if they are to do this, their lives must conform to the norms of faith that so imbued John Mary Vianney and enabled him to perform such wonderful works. "Oh, the wonderful faith of this priest"—one of his colleagues in the sacred ministry remarked—"It is great enough to enrich all the souls of the diocese!" [53]

42. This constant union with God is best achieved and preserved through the various practices of priestly piety; many of the more important of them, such as daily meditation, visits to the Blessed Sacrament, recitation of the Rosary, careful examination of conscience, the Church, in her wise and provident regulations, has made obligatory for priests.[54] As for the hours of the Office, priests have undertaken a serious obligation to the Church to recite them.[55]

43. The neglect of some of these rules may often be the reason why certain churchmen are caught up in the whirl of external affairs, gradually lose their feeling for sacred things and finally fall into serious difficulties when they are shorn of all spiritual protection and enticed by the attractions of this earthly life. John Mary Vianney on the contrary "never

---

[53] Cf. ibid., v. 227, p. 976.
[54] C.I.C., canon 125.
[55] Ibid., canon 135.

neglected his own salvation, no matter how busy he may have been with that of others".[56]

44. To use the words of St. Pius X: "We are sure of this much ... that a priest must be deeply devoted to the practice of prayer if he is to live up to his rank and fulfill his duties properly ... For a priest must be much more careful than others to obey the command of Christ: You must always pray. Paul was only reaffirming this when he advised, as he did so often: Be constant in prayer, ever on the watch to give thanks; pray without ceasing." [57] And We are more than happy to adopt as Our own the words that Our immediate predecessor offered priests as their password at the very beginning of his pontificate: "Pray, more and more, and pray more intensely." [58]

St. John Vianney's Devotion to the Eucharist

45. The devotion to prayer of St. John M. Vianney, who was to spend almost the whole of the last thirty years of his life in Church caring for the crowds of penitents who flocked to him, had one special characteristic—it was specially directed toward the Eucharist.

46. It is almost unbelievable how ardent his devotion to Christ hidden beneath the veils of the Eucharist really was. "He is the one"—he said—"Who has loved us so much; why shouldn't we love Him in return?" [59] He was devoted to the adorable Sacrament of the altar with a burning charity and his soul was drawn to the sacred Tabernacle by a heavenly force that could not be resisted.

[56] Cf. Archiv. Secret. Vat., v. 227, p. 36.
[57] Exhortation Haerent animo, Acta Pii X, IV, pp. 248–49.
[58] Discourse of June 24, 1939: AAS 31 (1939): 249.
[59] Cf. Archiv. Secret. Vat., v. 227, p. 1103.

47. This is how he taught his faithful to pray: "You do not need many words when you pray. We believe on faith that the good and gracious God is there in the tabernacle; we open our souls to Him; and feel happy that He allows us to come before Him; this is the best way to pray." [60] He did everything that there was to be done to stir up the reverence and love of the faithful for Christ hidden in the Sacrament of the Eucharist and to bring them to share in the riches of the divine Synaxis; the example of his devotion was ever before them. "To be convinced of this— witnesses tell us—all that was necessary was to see him carrying out the sacred ceremonies or simply to see him genuflect when he passed the tabernacle." [61]

Benefits from Eucharistic Prayer

48. As Our predecessor of immortal memory, Pius XII, has said—"The wonderful example of St. John Mary Vianney retains all of its force for our times." [62] For the lengthy prayer of a priest before the adorable Sacrament of the Altar has a dignity and an effectiveness that cannot be found elsewhere nor be replaced. And so when the priest adores Christ Our Lord and gives thanks to Him, or offers satisfaction for his own sins and those of others, or finally when he prays constantly that God keep special watch over the causes committed to his care, he is inflamed with a more ardent love for the Divine Redeemer to whom he has sworn allegiance and for those to whom he is devoting his pastoral care. And a devotion to the Eucharist that is ardent, constant and that carries over into works also has the effect of

[60] Cf. ibid., v. 227, p. 45.
[61] Cf. ibid., v. 227, p. 459.
[62] Cf. Message of June 25, 1956: AAS 48 (1956): 579.

nourishing and fostering the inner perfection of his soul and assuring him, as he carries out his apostolic duties, of an abundance of the supernatural powers that the strongest workers for Christ must have.

49. We do not want to skip over the benefits that accrue to the faithful themselves in this way, as they see the piety of their priests and are drawn by their example. For, as Our predecessor of happy memory, Pius XII, pointed out in a talk to the clergy of this dear city: "If you want the faithful who are entrusted to your care to pray willingly and well, you must give them an example and let them see you praying in church. A priest kneeling devoutly and reverently before the tabernacle, and pouring forth prayers to God with all his heart, is a wonderful example to the Christian people and serves as an inspiration." [63] The saintly Curé of Ars used all of these helps in carrying out his apostolic office, and without a doubt they are suitable to all times and places.

The Mass and the Priesthood

50. But never forget that the principal form of Eucharistic prayer is contained in the holy Sacrifice of the Altar. It is Our opinion that this point ought to be considered more carefully, Venerable Brethren, for it touches on a particularly important aspect of priestly life.

51. It is not Our intention at this time to enter upon a lengthy treatment of the Church's teaching on the priesthood and on the Eucharistic Sacrifice as it has been handed down from antiquity. Our predecessors Pius XI and Pius XII have done this in clear and important documents and We

---

[63] Cf. Discourse of March 13,1943: AAS 35 (1943): 114–15.

urge you to take pains to see to it that the priests and faithful entrusted to your care are very familiar with them. This will clear up the doubts of some; and correct the more daring statements that have sometimes been made in discussing these matters.

52. But We too hope to say something worthwhile in this matter by showing the principal reason why the holy Curé of Ars, who, as befits a hero, was most careful in fulfilling his priestly duties, really deserves to be proposed to those who have the care of souls as a model of outstanding virtue and to be honored by them as their heavenly patron. If it is obviously true that a priest receives his priesthood so as to serve at the altar and that he enters upon this office by offering the Eucharistic Sacrifice, then it is equally true that for as long as he lives as God's minister, the Eucharistic Sacrifice will be the source and origin of the holiness that he attains and of the apostolic activity to which he devotes himself. All of these things came to pass in the fullest possible way in the case of St. John Vianney.

53. For, if you give careful consideration to all of the activity of a priest, what is the main point of his apostolate if not seeing to it that wherever the Church lives, a people who are joined by the bonds of faith, regenerated by holy Baptism and cleansed of their faults will be gathered together around the sacred altar? It is then that the priest, using the sacred power he has received, offers the divine Sacrifice in which Jesus Christ renews the unique immolation which He completed on Calvary for the redemption of mankind and for the glory of His heavenly Father. It is then that the Christians who have gathered together, acting through the ministry of the priest, present the divine Victim and offer themselves to the supreme and eternal God as a "sacrifice,

living, holy, pleasing to God".[64] There it is that the people
of God are taught the doctrines and precepts of faith and
are nourished with the Body of Christ, and there it is that
they find a means to gain supernatural life, to grow in it,
and if need be to regain unity. And there besides, the Mystical Body of Christ, which is the Church, grows with spiritual increase throughout the world down to the end of
time.

54. It is only right and fitting to call the life of St. John
Vianney a priestly and pastoral one in an outstanding way,
because he spent more and more time in preaching the truths
of religion and cleansing souls of the stain of sin as the
years went by, and because he was mindful of the altar of
God in each and every act of his sacred ministry!

55. It is true of course that the holy Cure's fame made
great crowds of sinners flock to Ars, while many priests
experience great difficulty in getting the people committed
to their care to come to them at all, and then find that they
have to teach them the most elementary truths of Christian
doctrine just as if they were working in a missionary land.
But as important and sometimes as trying as these apostolic
labors may be, they should never be permitted to make
men of God forget the great importance of the goal which
they must always keep in view and which St. John Vianney
attained through dedicating himself completely to the main
works of the apostolic life in a tiny country church.

Personal Holiness and the Mass

56. This should be kept in mind, in particular: whatever a
priest may plan, resolve, or do to become holy, he will have

[64] Rom 12:1.

to draw, for example and for heavenly strength, upon the Eucharistic Sacrifice which he offers, just as the Roman Pontifical urges: "Be aware of what you are doing; imitate what you hold in your hands."

57. In this regard, We are pleased to repeat the words used by Our immediate predecessor of happy memory in the Apostolic Exhortation entitled *Menti Nostrae*: "Just as the whole life of Our Savior was pointed toward His sacrifice of Himself, so too the life of the priest, who must reproduce the image of Christ in himself, must become a pleasing sacrifice with Him and through Him and in Him. . . . And so it is not enough for him to celebrate the Eucharistic sacrifice, but in a very deep sense, he must live it; for in this way, he can draw from it the heavenly strength that will enable him to be profoundly transformed and to share in the expiatory life of the Divine Redeemer himself. . . ." [65] And again: "The soul of the priest must refer what takes place on the sacrificial altar to himself; for just as Jesus Christ immolates Himself, his minister must immolate himself along with Him; just as Jesus expiates the sins of men, so too the priest must tread the lofty path of Christian asceticism to bring about his own purification and that of his neighbors." [66]

Safeguarding Holiness

58. This lofty aspect of doctrine is what the Church has in mind when, with maternal care, she invites her sacred ministers to devote themselves to asceticism and urges them to celebrate the Eucharistic Sacrifice with the greatest possible interior and exterior devotion. May not the fact that some

[65] Apostolic exhortation *Menti Nostrae*, AAS 42 (1950): 666–67.
[66] Cf. ibid., 667–68.

priests fail to keep in mind the close connection that ought
to exist between the offering of the Sacrifice and their own
self-dedication be the reason why they gradually fall off from
that first fervor they had at the time of their ordination? St.
John Vianney learned this from experience and expressed it
this way: "The reason why priests are remiss in their personal lives is that they do not offer the Sacrifice with attention and piety." And he, who in his lofty virtue, was in the
habit of "offering himself as an expiation for sinners" [67] used
to weep "when he thought of the unhappy priests who did
not measure up to the holiness demanded by their office".[68]

59. Speaking as a Father, We urge Our beloved priests to
set aside a time to examine themselves on how they celebrate the divine mysteries, what their dispositions of soul and
external attitude are as they ascend the altar and what fruit
they are trying to gain from it. They should be spurred to do
this by the centenary celebrations that are being held in honor
of this outstanding and wonderful priest, who drew such great
strength and such great desire to dedicate himself "from the
consolation and happiness of offering the divine victim".[69]
May his prayers, which We feel sure they will have, bring a
fullness of light and strength down upon Our beloved priests.

III

60. The wonderful examples of priestly asceticism and prayer
that We have proposed for your consideration up to now,
Venerable Brethren, also point clearly to the source of the
pastoral skill and of the truly remarkable heavenly effectiveness of the sacred ministry of St. John M. Vianney. In this

[67] Cf. *Archiv. Secret. Vat.*, v. 227, p. 319.
[68] Cf. ibid., v. 227, p. 47.
[69] Cf. ibid., pp. 667–68.

regard, Our predecessor of happy memory, Pius XII, gave
a wise warning: "The priest should realize that the important ministry entrusted to him will be more fruitfully carried out, the more intimately he is united with Christ
and led on by His spirit." [70] As a matter of fact, the life
of the Curé of Ars offers one more outstanding argument
in support of the supreme rule for apostolic labor that was
laid down by Jesus Christ Himself: "Without me, you can
do nothing." [71]

The Good Shepherd

61. We have no intention of trying to make a list of all the
wonderful things done by this humble Curé of a country
parish, who drew such immense crowds to the tribunal of
Penance that some people, out of contempt, called him "a
kind of nineteenth-century rabble-rouser"; [72] nor do We see
any need of going into all of the particular ways in which
he carried out his duties, some of which, perhaps, could
not be accommodated to our times.

62. But We do want to recall this one fact—that this
Saint was in his own times a model of pastoral devotion in
a tiny community that was still suffering from the loss of
Christian faith and morals that occurred while the French
Revolution was raging. This was the mission and command
received just before taking over his pastoral office: "You will
find love of God in that parish; stir it up yourself." [73]

63. He proved to be a tireless worker for God, one who
was wise and devoted in winning over young people and

---

[70] Apostolic exhortation *Menti Nostrae*, AAS 42 (1950): 676.
[71] John 15:5.
[72] Cf. *Archiv. Secret. Vat.*, v. 227, p. 629.
[73] Cf. ibid., v. 227, p. 15.

bringing families back to the standards of Christian morality, a worker who was never too tired to show an interest in the human needs of his flock, one whose own way of life was very close to theirs and who was prepared to exert every effort and make any sacrifice to establish Christian schools and to make missions available to the people: and all of these things show that St. John M. Vianney reproduced the true image of the good shepherd in himself as he dealt with the flock entrusted to his care, for he knew his sheep, protected them from dangers, and gently but firmly looked after them.

64. Without realizing it, he was sounding his own praises in the words he once addressed to his people: "Good shepherd! O shepherd who lives up to the commands and desires of Jesus Christ completely! This is the greatest blessing that a kind and gracious God can send to a parish." [74]

65. But there are three things in particular of lasting value and importance that the example of this holy man brings home to us and it is to these in particular that We would like to direct your attention, Venerable Brethren.

His Esteem for the Pastoral Office

66. The first thing that strikes Us is the very high esteem in which he held his pastoral office. He was so humble by disposition and so much aware through faith of the importance of the salvation of a human soul that he could never undertake his parish duties without a feeling of fear.

67. "My friend"—these are the words he used to open his heart to a fellow-priest—"you have no idea of how fearful a thing it is for a priest to be snatched away from

---

[74] Cf. *Sermons*, 1.c., v. 2, p. 86.

the care of souls to appear before the judgment seat of God." [75]

68. Everyone knows—as We have already pointed out—how much he yearned and how long he prayed to be allowed to go off by himself to weep and to make proper expiation for what he called his miserable life; and We also know that only obedience and his zeal for the salvation of others got him to return to the field of the apostolate when he had abandoned it.

Sufferings for His Sheep

69. But if he felt the great weight of this burden to be so heavy that it sometimes seemed to be crushing him, this was also the reason why he conceived his office and its duties in so lofty a fashion that carrying them out called for great strength of soul. These are the prayers he addressed to heaven as he began his parochial ministry: "My God, make the sheep entrusted to me come back to a good way of life. For all my life I am prepared to endure anything that pleases you." [76]

70. And God heard these fervent prayers, for later our saint had to confess: "If I had known when I came to the parish of Ars what I would have to suffer, the fear of it would certainly have killed me." [77]

71. Following in the footsteps of the great apostles of all ages, he knew that the best and most effective way for him to contribute to the salvation of those who would be entrusted to his care was through the cross. It was for them that he put up with all sorts of calumnies, prejudices and opposition, without complaint; for them that he willingly

---

[75] Cf. *Archiv. Secret. Vat.*, v. 227 p. 1210.
[76] Cf. *Archiv. Secret. Vat.*, v. 227 p. 53.
[77] Cf. ibid., v. 227, p. 991.

endured the sharp discomforts and annoyances of mind and body that were forced upon him by his daily administration of the Sacrament of Penance for thirty years with almost no interruption; for them that this athlete of Christ fought off the powers of hell; for them, last of all, that he brought his body into subjection through voluntary mortification.

72. Almost everyone knows his answer to the priest who complained to him that his apostolic zeal was bearing no fruit: "You have offered humble prayers to God, you have wept, you have groaned, you have sighed. Have you added fasts, vigils, sleeping on the floor, castigation of your body? Until you have done all of these, do not think that you have tried everything." [78]

Need for Comparison

73. Once again Our mind turns to sacred ministers who have the care of souls, and We urgently beg them to realize the importance of these words. Let each one think over his own life, in the light of the supernatural prudence that should govern all of our actions, and ask himself if it is really all that the pastoral care of the people entrusted to him requires.

74. With firm confidence that the merciful God will never fail to offer the help that human weakness calls for, let sacred ministers think over the offices and burdens they have assumed by looking at St. John M. Vianney as if he were a mirror. "A terrible disaster strikes us Curés"—the holy man complained—"when our spirit grows lazy and careless"; he was referring to the harmful attitude of those pastors who are not disturbed by the fact that many sheep committed to them are growing filthy in the slavery of sin. If they want to imitate the Curé of Ars more closely, who was so

[78] Cf. ibid., v. 227, p. 53.

"convinced that men should be loved, so that we can do
good to them",[79] then let these priests ask themselves what
kind of love they have for those whom God has entrusted
to their care and for whom Christ has died!

75. Because of human liberty and of events beyond all
human control, the efforts of even the holiest of men will
sometimes fail. But a priest ought to remember that in the
mysterious counsels of Divine Providence, the eternal fate
of many men is bound up with his pastoral interest and
care and the example of his priestly life. Is not this thought
powerful enough both to stir up the lackadaisical in an effective way and to urge on to greater efforts those who are
already zealous in the work of Christ?

Preacher and Catechist

76. Because, as is recorded, "he was always ready to care
for the needs of souls",[80] St. John M. Vianney, good shepherd that he was, was also outstanding in offering his sheep
an abundant supply of the food of Christian truth. Throughout his life, he preached and taught Catechism.

77. The Council of Trent pronounced this to be a parish
priest's first and greatest duty and everyone knows what
immense and constant labor John Vianney expended in order
to be equal to carrying out this task. For he began his course
of studies when he was already along in years, and he had
great difficulty with it; and his first sermons to the people
kept him up for whole nights on end. How much the ministers of the word of God can find here to imitate! For
there are some who give up all effort at further study and

---

[79] Cf. *Archiv. Secret. Vat.*, v. 227, p. 1002.
[80] Cf. ibid., v. 227, p. 580.

then point too readily to his small fund of learning as an adequate excuse for themselves. They would be much better off if they would imitate the great perseverance of soul with which the Curé of Ars prepared himself to carry out this great ministry to the best of his abilities: which, as a matter of fact, were not quite as limited as is sometimes believed, for he had a clear mind and sound judgment.[81]

Obligation to Learn

78. Men in Sacred Orders should gain an adequate knowledge of human affairs and a thorough knowledge of sacred doctrine that is in keeping with their abilities. Would that all pastors of souls would exert as much effort as the Curé of Ars did to overcome difficulties and obstacles in learning, to strengthen memory through practice, and especially to draw knowledge from the Cross of Our Lord, which is the greatest of all books. This is why his Bishop made this reply to some of his critics: "I do not know whether he is learned; but a heavenly light shines in him."[82]

Model for Preachers

79. This is why Our predecessor of happy memory, Pius XII, was perfectly right in not hesitating to offer this country Cure as a model for the preachers of the Holy City: "The holy Curé of Ars had none of the natural gifts of a speaker that stand out in men like P. Segneri or B. Bossuet. But the clear, lofty, living thoughts of his mind were reflected in the sound of his voice and shone forth from his glance, and they came out in the form of ideas

---

[81] Cf. *Archiv. Secret Vat.*, v. 3897, p. 444.
[82] Cf. ibid., v. 3897, p. 272.

and images that were so apt and so well fitted to the thoughts and feelings of his listeners and so full of wit and charm that even St. Francis de Sales would have been struck with admiration. This is the kind of speaker who wins the souls of the faithful. A man who is filled with Christ will not find it hard to discover ways and means of bringing others to Christ." [83]

80. These words give a wonderful picture of the Curé of Ars as a catechism teacher and as a preacher. And when, towards the end of his life on earth, his voice was too weak to carry to his listeners, the sparkle and gleam of his eyes, his tears, his sighs of divine love, the bitter sorrow he evidenced when the mere concept of sin came to his mind, were enough to convert to a better way of life the faithful who surrounded his pulpit. How could anyone help being moved deeply with a life so completely dedicated to Christ shining so clearly there before him?

81. Up to the time of his blessed death, St. John M. Vianney held on tenaciously to his office of teaching the faithful committed to his care and the pious pilgrims who crowded the church, by denouncing evil of every kind, in whatever guise it might appear, "in season, out of season" [84] and, even more, by sublimely raising souls to God; for "he preferred to show the beauties of virtue rather than the ugliness of vice." [85] For this humble priest understood perfectly how great the dignity and sublimity of teaching the word of God really is. "Our Lord"—he said—"who Himself is truth, has as much regard for His word as for His Body."

---

[83] Cf. Discourse of March 16, 1946: AAS 38 (1946): 186.

[84] 2 Tim 4:2.

[85] Cf. *Archiv. Secret. Vat.*, v. 227, p. 185.

The Obligation to Teach

82. So it is easy to realize what great joy it brought Our predecessors to point out an example like this to be imitated by those who guide the Christian people; for the proper and careful exercise of the teaching office by the clergy is of great importance. In speaking of this, St. Pius X had this to say: "We want especially to pursue this one point and to urge strongly that no priest has any more important duty or is bound by any stricter obligation." [86]

83. And so once again We take this warning which Our predecessors have repeated over and over again and which has been inserted in the Code of Canon Law as well,[87] and We issue it to you, Venerable Brethren, on the occasion of the solemn celebration of the centenary of the holy catechist and preacher of Ars.

84. In this regard We wish to offer Our praise and encouragement to the studies that have been carefully and prudently carried on in many areas under your leadership and auspices, to improve the religious training of both youngsters and adults by presenting it in a variety of forms that are specially adapted to local circumstances and needs. All of these efforts are useful; but on the occasion of this centenary, God wants to cast new light on the wonderful power of the apostolic spirit, that sweeps all in its path, as it is exemplified in this priest who throughout his life was a witness in word and deed for Christ nailed to the cross "not in the persuasive language devised by human wisdom, but in a manifestation of spiritual power".[88]

[86] Encyclical letter *Acerbo nimis, Acta Pii* X, II, p. 75.
[87] C.I.C. canons 1330–32.
[88] 1 Cor 2:4

His Ministry in the Confessional

85. All that remains for Us to do is to recall at a little greater
length the pastoral ministry of St. John M. Vianney, which
was a kind of steady martyrdom for a long period of his
life, and especially his administration of the sacrament of
Penance, which calls for special praise for it brought forth
the richest and most salutary fruits.

86. "For almost fifteen hours each day, he lent a patient
ear to penitents. This work began early in the morning and
continued well on into the night." [89] And when he was
completely worn out and broken five days before his death
and had no strength left, the final penitents came to his
bed. Toward the end of his life, the number of those who
came to see him each year reached eighty thousand according to the accounts.[90]

His Anguish Over Sins

87. It is hard to imagine what pain and discomfort and bodily
sufferings this man underwent as he sat to hear Confessions
in the tribunal of Penance for what seemed like endless peri-
ods of time, especially if you recall how weakened he was by
his fasts, mortifications, sicknesses, vigils and lack of sleep.

88. But he was bothered even more by a spiritual anguish
that took complete possession of him. Listen to his mourn-
ful cries: "So many crimes against God are committed"—he
said—"that they sometimes incline us to ask God to end
this world! ... You have to come to the town of Ars if you
really want to learn what an infinite multitude of serious
sins there are.... Alas, we do not know what to do, we

[89] Cf. *Archiv. Secret. Vat.*, v. 227, p. 18.
[90] Cf. ibid.

think that there is nothing else to do than weep and pray to God."

89. And this holy man could have added that he had taken on himself more than his share of the expiation of these sins. For he told those who asked his advice in this regard: "I impose only a small penance on those who confess their sins properly; the rest I perform in their place." [91]

His Concern for Sinners

90. St. John M. Vianney always had "poor sinners", as he called them, in his mind and before his eyes, with the constant hope of seeing them turn back to God and weep for the sins they had committed. This was the object of all his thoughts and cares, and of the work that took up almost all his time and efforts. [92]

91. From his experience in the tribunal of Penance, in which he loosed the bonds of sin, he understood just how much malice there is in sin and what terrible devastation it wreaks in the souls of men. He used to paint it in hideous colors: "If we"—he asserted—"had the faith to see a soul in mortal sin, we would die of fright." [93]

92. But the sufferings of souls who have remained attached to their sins in hell did not add to the strength and vigor of his own sorrow and words as much as did the anguish he felt at the fact that divine love had been carelessly neglected or violated by some offense. This stubbornness in sin and ungrateful disregard for God's great goodness made rivers

[91] Cf. *Archiv. Secret. Vat.*, v. 227, p. 1018.
[92] Cf. ibid., v. 227, p. 18.
[93] Cf. ibid., v. 227, p. 290.

of tears flow from his eyes. "My friend"—he said—"I am weeping because you are not." [94]

93. And yet, what great kindness he displayed in devoting himself to restoring hope to the souls of repentant sinners! He spared no effort to become a minister of divine mercy to them; and he described it as "like an overflowing river that carries all souls along with it" [95] and throbs with a love greater than that of a mother, "for God is quicker to forgive than a mother to snatch her child from the fire." [96]

The Seriousness of Confession

94. Let the example of the Curé of Ars stir up those who are in charge of souls to be eager and well-prepared in devoting themselves to this very serious work, for it is here most of all that divine mercy finally triumphs over human malice and that men have their sins wiped away and are reconciled to God.

95. And let them also remember that Our predecessor of happy memory, Pius XII, expressed disapproval "in the strongest terms" of the opinion of those who have little use for frequent confession, where it is a matter of venial sins; the Supreme Pontiff said: "We particularly recommend the pious practice of frequent confession, which the Church has introduced, under the influence of the Holy Spirit, as a means of swifter daily progress along the road of virtue." [97]

96. Again, We have complete confidence that sacred ministers will be even more careful than others in faithfully

---

[94] Cf. ibid., v. 227, p. 999.
[95] Cf. ibid., v. 227, p. 978.
[96] Cf. ibid., v. 3900, p. 1554.
[97] Encyclical letter *Mystici Corporis*, AAS 35 (1943): 235.

observing the prescriptions of Canon Law,[98] which make the pious use of the Sacrament of Penance, which is so necessary for the attainment of sanctity, obligatory at certain specified times; and that they will treat those urgent exhortations which this same predecessor of Ours made "with a sorrowful soul" on several occasions[99] with the supreme veneration and obedience they deserve.

Necessity of Personal Holiness

97. As this Encyclical of Ours draws to a close, We want to assure you, Venerable Brethren, of the high hopes We have that these centenary celebrations will, with the help of God, lead to a deeper desire and more intensive efforts on the part of all priests to carry out their sacred ministry with more ardent zeal and especially to work to fulfill "the first duty of priests, that is, the duty of becoming holy themselves".[100]

98. When We gaze from this height of the Supreme Pontificate to which We have been raised by the secret counsels of Divine Providence and turn Our mind to what souls are hoping for and expecting, or to the many areas of the earth that have not yet been brightened by the light of the Gospel, or last of all to the many needs of the Christian people, the figure of the priest is always before Our eyes.

99. If there were no priests or if they were not doing their daily work, what use would all these apostolic undertakings be, even those which seem best suited to the present

---

[98] C.I.C. canon 125, section 1.

[99] Cf. encyclical letter *Mystici Corporis*, AAS 35 (1943): 235; encyclical letter *Mediator Dei*, AAS 39 (1947): 585; apostolic exhortation *Menti Nostrae*, AAS 42 (1950): 674.

[100] Apostolic Exhortation *Menti Nostrae*, AAS 42 (1950): 677.

age? Of what use would be the laymen who work so zealously and generously to help in the activities of the apostolate?

100. And so We do not hesitate to speak to all of these
sacred ministers, whom We love so much and in whom the
Church rests such great hopes—these priests—and urge them
in the name of Jesus Christ from the depths of a father's
heart to be faithful in doing and giving all that the seri-
ousness of their ecclesiastical dignity requires of them.

101. This appeal of Ours draws added force from the
wise and prudent words of St. Pius X: "Nothing is needed
more to promote the kingdom of Jesus Christ in the world
than the holiness of churchmen, who should stand out
above the faithful by their example, their words and their
teaching." [101]

102. And this fits in perfectly with the words that St.
John M. Vianney addressed to his bishop: "If you want the
whole diocese to be converted to God, then all of the Curés
must become holy."

Help From Bishops

103. And We especially want to commend these most beloved
sons to you, Venerable Brethren, who bear the chief responsibility for the holiness of your clergy, so that you will be
careful to go to them and help them in the difficulties—
sometimes serious ones—that they face in their own lives
or in carrying out their duties.

104. What is there that cannot be accomplished by a bishop
who loves the clergy entrusted to his direction, who is close
to them, really knows them, takes great care of them and
directs them in a firm but fatherly way?

---

[101] Cf. epistle "*La ristorazione*", *Acta Pii X*, 1, p. 257.

105. It is true that your pastoral care is supposed to extend to the whole diocese, but you should still take very special care of those who are in sacred orders, for they are your closest helpers in your work and are bound to you by many sacred ties.

Help From the Faithful

106. On the occasion of this centenary celebration, We would also like to exhort paternally all of the faithful to offer constant prayers to God for their priests, so that each in his own way may help them attain holiness.

107. Those who are more fervent and devout are turning their eyes and their minds to the priest with a great deal of hope and expectation. For, at a time when you find flourishing everywhere the power of money, the allure of pleasures of the senses, and too great an esteem for technical achievements, they want to see in him a man who speaks in the name of God, who is animated by a firm faith, and who gives no thought to himself, but burns with intense charity.

108. So let them all realize that they can help sacred ministers a great deal to achieve this lofty goal, if only they will show due respect for priestly dignity, and have proper esteem for their pastoral office and its difficulties, and finally be even more zealous and active in offering to help them.

A Call for Vocations

109. We cannot help turning our paternal spirit in a special way to young people; We embrace them with a warm love and remind them that, in them, the Church rests great hopes for the years to come.

110. The harvest indeed is great, but the laborers are few.[102] How many areas there are where the heralds of the Gospel truth are worn out by their labors and waiting eagerly and longingly for those to come who will take their place! There are peoples who are languishing in a miserable hunger for heavenly food more than for earthly nourishment. Who will bring the heavenly banquet of life and truth to them?

111. We have complete confidence that the youngsters of our time will be as quick as those of times past to give a generous answer to the invitation of the Divine Master to provide for this vital need.

112. Priests often find themselves in difficult circumstances. This is not surprising; for those who hate the Church always show their hostility by trying to harm and deceive her sacred ministers; as the Curé of Ars himself admitted, those who want to overthrow religion always try in their hatred to strike at priests first of all.

113. But even in the face of these serious difficulties, priests who are ardent in their devotion to God enjoy a real, sublime happiness from an awareness of their own position, for they know that they have been called by the Divine Savior to offer their help in a most holy work, which will have an effect on the redemption of the souls of men and on the growth of the Mystical Body of Christ. So let Christian families consider it one of their most sublime privileges to give priests to the Church; and so let them offer their sons to the sacred ministry with joy and gratitude.

Lourdes and Ars

114. There is no need to dwell on this point, Venerable Brothers, since what We are urging is very close to your

---

[102] Cf. Matt 9:37.

own hearts. For We are sure that you understand perfectly Our interest in these things and the forceful expression We are giving to it, and that you share it. For the present, We commit this matter of immense importance, closely bound up with the salvation of many souls, to the intercession of St. John M. Vianney.

115. We also turn Our eyes to the Mother of God, immaculate from the very beginning. Shortly before the Curé of Ars, filled with heavenly merits, completed his long life, She appeared in another part of France to an innocent and humble girl, and through her, invited men with a mother's insistence to devote themselves to prayers and Christian penance; this majestic voice is still striking home to souls a century later, and echoing far and wide almost endlessly.

116. The things that were done and said by this holy priest, who was raised to the honors of the Heavenly Saints and whose 100th anniversary We are commemorating, cast a kind of heavenly light beforehand over the supernatural truths which were made known to the innocent girl at the grotto of Lourdes. For this man had such great devotion to the Immaculate Conception of the Virgin Mother of God that in 1836 he dedicated his parish church to Mary Conceived Without Sin and greeted the infallible definition of this truth as Catholic dogma in 1854 with the greatest joy and reverence.[103]

117. So there is good reason for Us to link together this double centenary, of Lourdes and of Ars, as We give proper thanks to the most high God: each supplements the other, and each does honor to a nation We love very much and which can boast of having both of these most holy places in its bosom.

[103] Cf. *Archiv. Secret. Vat.*, v. 227, p. 90.

118. Mindful of the many benefits that have been received, and trusting confidently that still more will come to Us and to the whole Church, We borrow the prayer that sounded so often on the lips of the Curé of Ars: "Blessed be the most holy and immaculate conception of the Blessed Virgin Mary, Mother of God. May all nations praise, all lands invoke and preach your Immaculate Heart!" [104]

119. Confident that this centennial celebration of St. John M. Vianney throughout the world will stir up the pious zeal of priests and of those whom God is calling to take up the priesthood, and will make all the faithful even more active and interested in supplying the things that are needed for priests' life and work, with all Our heart We impart the Apostolic Blessing to each and every one of them, and especially to you, Venerable Brethren, as a consoling pledge of heavenly graces and of Our good will.

Given at Rome, at St. Peter's, on 1 August 1959, the first year of Our Pontificate.

JOHN XXIII

[104] Cf. ibid., v. 227, p. 1021.

4

Novena to St. John Vianney
By the Reverend Anthony J. Manuppella

INTRODUCTION

It is the wish of the author that devotion to St. John Vianney will grow by means of this novena. May it aid all priests and seminarians to grow in holiness through the intercession of their heavenly patron. Through this novena, may all Catholics be given the greatest of gifts—holy priests. May the laity direct their prayers in this novena especially to obtain good and holy priests for the Church.

May Mary, the Mother of priests, and her faithful son, St. John Marie Vianney, bless the apostolate of praying for all those who have dedicated their lives to God and the Church.

FIRST DAY
St. John Vianney, who accepted the cross

"If any man would come after me, let him deny himself and take up his cross and follow me." (Mt 16:24)

O holy priest of Ars, as a young seminarian you encountered many obstacles on the road to the priesthood, but you realized that to suffer was to suffer with Christ on Calvary.

Knowing that if following your Lord meant taking up His cross, you lovingly embraced it. Your motto in life became: love while suffering and suffer in order to love. You did not get discouraged; rather, your strong faith united you more with Jesus every day of your life.

O great St. John Vianney, you know what is needed for my salvation: a strong faith able to accept the will of God in all things. If I want to serve Christ, I too must take up my cross and follow Him. By your prayers, obtain for me a heart full of courage and strength; obtain for your priests, religious, and seminarians that same courage and strength to follow Jesus whole-heartedly, even if it means following Him to Calvary. Intercede for me before the Lord that I may do the will of God, obey the commandments, and loyally love the Church, the Bride of Christ.

NOVENA PRAYER

O holy priest of Ars, St. John Marie Vianney, you loved God and served Him faithfully as His priest. Now you see God face to face in heaven. You never despaired but persevered in your faith until your death. Remember now the dangers, fears and anxieties that surround me and intercede for me in all my needs and troubles, especially (mention your request). O St. John Vianney, I have confidence in your intercession. Pray for me in a special way during this novena.

SECOND DAY
St. John Vianney, full of zeal for souls

"For what will it profit a man if he gains the whole world and forfeits his life?
Or what shall a man give in return for his life?" (Mt 16:26)

O holy priest of Ars, you taught men to pray daily: "O my God, come to me, so that You may dwell in me and I may dwell in You." Your life was the living out of this prayer. The divine life of grace abided in you. Your zeal for the salvation of souls manifested itself in your total self-surrender to God expressed in your selfless service to others. You gave of yourself unreservedly in the confessional, at the altar, in the classroom, and in every action you performed.

O great St. John Vianney, obtain for me the realization that when I am free of mortal sin God dwells also in me. I know that the salvation of my soul is the fulfillment of my existence. Awaken in me a sense of self-giving for the salvation of souls. By your intercession obtain for all priests, religious, and seminarians a zeal for souls like your zeal. May they see that God dwells in them and in their fellow men. Obtain for them from our Lord the grace to lead all men to salvation. Let them take up your challenge: "If you really love God, you will greatly desire to see Him loved by all the world."

Recite the novena prayer.

THIRD DAY
St. John Vianney, adorer of the Blessed Sacrament

"Truly, truly, I say to you, unless you eat the flesh of the Son of man and drink his blood, you have no life in you. . . . He who eats my flesh and drinks my blood abides in me, and I in him." (Jn 6:53, 56)

O holy priest of Ars, you had such an overwhelming love for Christ in the Blessed Sacrament that you prayed for hours in His presence. You said that "when our Lord sees them coming eagerly to visit Him in the Blessed Sacrament, He smiles upon them. They come with that simplicity which pleases Him so much."

O saint of the Eucharist, may your example enkindle in me a love for Jesus in the Blessed Sacrament. By your prayers, never let me doubt Christ's Real Presence, but obtain for me a firm faith rooted in Him. Help me not to be afraid to defend or preach Christ's Real Presence in the Blessed Sacrament. Obtain for me the grace to approach our Lord with simplicity of heart as I lay my soul's innermost thoughts before His Sacred Heart. Keep priests, religious, and seminarians under your continual protection that they may be supported by your example and assistance and be faithfully devoted to Christ in the Blessed Sacrament. May their lives reflect their belief in our Lord's abiding presence with us. O St. John Vianney, by the power of your intercession, give us priests devoted to the holy Sacrament of the Altar.

Recite the novena prayer.

FOURTH DAY

St. John Vianney, greatly devoted to our Blessed Mother

"O daughter, you are blessed by the Most High God above all women on earth; and blessed be the Lord God, who created the heavens and the earth." (Judith 13:18)

O holy priest of Ars, your life was consecrated to the Blessed Mother. You prayed earnestly to her, entrusting your priesthood to her care. You begged all the faithful to pray the rosary, the favorite prayer of Mary, our Mother. You summed up the reason for your great love of our Lady by saying: "We have only to turn to the Blessed Mother to be heard. Her heart is all love."

O great St. John Vianney, I ask you with all my heart, through the merits of Jesus and the intercession of Mary, the Virgin Mother, to make my life patterned after that of our heavenly Mother, full of love for God and my neighbor. Obtain for me a deep love for our Lady and a filial confidence in her. She is the person to whom I can turn in times of distress, loneliness, anger, or temptation. Inspire priests, religious, and seminarians to consecrate their lives to their Mother in heaven. May priests throughout the world never desert the Cross of Christ but remain, as Mary did, at the foot of the Cross.

Recite the novena prayer.

FIFTH DAY
St. John Vianney, lover of sinners

"Come to me, all who labor and are heavy laden, and I will give you rest. Take my yoke upon you, and learn from me; for I am gentle and lowly in heart, and you will find rest for your souls. For my yoke is easy, and my burden is light." (Mt 11:28–30)

O holy priest of Ars, you daily spent many long hours in the confessional. People came to you for forgiveness of their sins from far-off places. Although you despised sin, you always received the sinner with much love and forgiveness.

O holy confessor of the Lord, St. John Vianney, awaken in me a sense of my sinfulness before the eyes of God. By your priestly example and prayers, grant me a love of the sacrament of Penance. Obtain for me the understanding that it is in confessing my sins that God's mercy is poured out upon me and that I draw closer to Christ. Obtain for me a deep hatred of sin and the grace to resist temptation. Teach me the value of frequent confession, where I meet Jesus my Savior, the source of all mercy and consolation. Pray that all priests, religious, and seminarians may always love the sacrament of Penance. Pray that they may call sinners to repentance by the example of their lives given in complete service to our Lord.

Recite the novena prayer.

SIXTH DAY
St. John Vianney, model of purity

"Let no one despise [you], but set the believers an example in speech and conduct, in love, in faith, in purity."
(1 Tim 4:12)

O holy priest of Ars, your life was a model of purity. Your life of chastity was a source of edification to all. You said that when a soul is pure all the court of heaven looks upon it with great joy. Today we are experiencing a great disregard for the virtue of purity; it is looked upon with ridicule by worldly standards.

O great St. John Vianney, more than ever before I need your prayers and help in avoiding sins of impurity. I ask you to help me keep pure in mind and in body and to be a good example in my speech, conduct, and faith. Obtain for me the strength necessary to combat temptations against the virtue of purity, which would lead me away from God. Unite your prayers with those of Mary Immaculate to implore God that all priests, religious, and seminarians be pure in mind and heart and be preserved from those sins which are so displeasing to God.

Recite the novena prayer.

SEVENTH DAY
St. John Vianney, humble in all things

"Whoever exalts himself will be humbled, and whoever humbles himself will be exalted." (Mt 23:12)

O holy priest of Ars, your life was filled with humility. You wore an old cassock; you ate meager meals. You realized that before the throne of God you were one of His creatures, made to glorify God and to praise Him in all things. You said that "the first virtue is humility; the second, humility; and the third, humility." You counseled people to remain humble, remain simple; the more humble and simple one is, the more good he will do. Your simplicity of soul and your uncluttered way of life led you to sanctity.

O humble St. John Vianney, when I forget that I am totally dependent on God for everything, intercede for me with Almighty God. Allow me to see that without my Creator nothing is possible and that I must rely on God for everything. He is my Creator, who keeps me in existence at every moment. Obtain for all priests, religious, and seminarians the grace of humility. May their lives exemplify your humility and simplicity, a life uncluttered, a life totally dependent on God.

Recite the novena prayer.

EIGHTH DAY

St. John Vianney, lover of penance and mortification

"If the world hates you, know that it has hated me before it hated you." (Jn 15:18)

O holy priest of Ars, you led a life of detachment from worldly pleasures. You fasted every day; you slept a few hours each night. You did all of this so that you would be able to serve God to the best of your ability. Your life portrayed this saying: "We complain when we suffer. We have much more reason to complain when we do not suffer, since nothing so likens us to our Lord as the bearing of His Cross."

O great St. John Vianney, in these days when we are surrounded by so many comforts and pleasures, it can be so difficult for us to do penance for our sins and live a life of detachment. I resolve to offer some sacrifice today for the expiation of my sins and the sins of all mankind. I resolve lovingly to accept the cross God chooses to send me. May all priests, religious, and seminarians become men and women of sacrifice. May they willingly offer their whole lives to God! Obtain for them the grace to liken their lives to that of Christ by the bearing of His Cross.

Recite the novena prayer.

NINTH DAY
St. John Vianney, good and holy priest

"As therefore you received Christ Jesus the Lord, so live in him, rooted and built up in him and established in the faith, just as you were taught, abounding in thanksgiving." (Col 2:6–7)

O holy priest of Ars, you lived in an age of much upheaval, in a time when men turned their backs on God. Your bishop told you of a parish to which he wished to send you where there was no love. He assigned you to Ars and said that you would be their priest, the one who would show the people the love of God. Not only did you draw these people back to God, but your saintly reputation soon spread and converted many people to a life of holiness. You said that a good priest, a priest after Christ's own heart, is the greatest treasure that God can give a parish. Ask God to give us such priests!

O great St. John Vianney, once again we are living in days of upheaval. There is much evil in the world. Obtain for me the grace to persevere in my faith and never to despair. May I walk with the Lord and trust in Him all the days of my life. Obtain through your heavenly intercession—for all priests, religious, and seminarians—the grace of modeling their lives after that of Jesus Christ. We need, more than ever, priests full of the love of God, able to bring the world to Christ. Pray for good priests, O great priest of Ars.

Recite the novena prayer.

Imprimatur:
   † Most Reverend George H. Guilfoyle
   Bishop of Camden

   February 13, 1975

Grateful acknowledgment is made to Templegate Publishers, Springfield, Illinois, for the kind permission granted to reprint quotations from *Thoughts of the Curé of Ars.*

Scripture passages from Revised Standard version, second Catholic Edition. All rights reserved.

Novena © 1975. (Copyrighted in 1975 by the Daughters of St. Paul. All rights reserved.) Reprinted by kind permission of Anthony Manuppella.